PETRUS BOREL
THE LYCANTHROPE

PETRUS BOREL
From the lithograph by Célestin Nanteuil
after the portrait by Louis Boulanger

PETRUS BOREL
THE LYCANTHROPE

His Life and Times

by

ENID STARKIE

FABER AND FABER LIMITED
24 Russell Square
London

First published in mcmliv
by Faber and Faber Limited
24 Russell Square London W.C.1
Printed in Great Britain by
R. MacLehose and Company Limited
The University Press Glasgow

For
SARAH WATSON
in whose little house
in the Forest of Fontainebleau
this book was largely written

CONTENTS

CONTENTS
Appendixes

ILLUSTRATIONS

INTRODUCTION

Most readers of French poetry see Baudelaire as standing solitary on a lonely peak of nineteenth-century literature, owing no debt to anyone and sharing, as far as can be seen, few similarities with the other great poets of his age. Yet poets are never born through self-generation, nor do they spin their poetry from their own substance alone. There is always some seed which fertilises their own particular genius, some special impetus which urges them to write. If the well mapped-out highways of French poetry are forsaken and the by-ways explored, then the source of much that is considered most characteristically Baudelairean will be encountered, discovered in a minor, now almost forgotten, school of poets which flourished in the early years of the July Monarchy, a school born of the Revolution of 1830 and conceived during the troubled years which preceded it. It lasted for a short time only, from 1830 to 1835, being eventually crushed beneath the weight of the new bourgeois régime when it was finally accepted in the later eighteen-thirties. Baudelaire becomes intelligible—especially the early Baudelaire—when the significance of this group of writers is realised. They are moreover important, not only for the better appreciation of Baudelaire himself, but also for the fuller understanding of their age and of such later poets as Corbière, Lautréamont and Rimbaud, as well as the Surrealist writers.

The reign of Louis Philippe was one of the most prosaic periods in French history, a time when material values, generally speaking, alone prevailed, and there were immense prizes for those who could gain the ears of the new and powerful middle class. There were some however who considered that this bid for popularity could only result in the adulteration of the pure standards of good taste. They, for their part, took a pride in their lack of popularity and were the first men of letters to isolate themselves from the general public as if from contamination. They refused to bow to the prevailing wind and thought that an artist could not, without prostituting his art, appeal to the masses. The leader of this exclusive group of poets of the eighteen-thirties was Petrus Borel who styled himself the Lycanthrope, that is the man-wolf.

Although Petrus Borel does not figure in the first flight of the most memorable French poets, he is more interesting as an artist and more originally experimental than many of the greatest masters, also more subtle as a personality. He was moreover one of the most striking and spectacular figures in his own day and in him can be clearly discerned the artistic ideals of the time. It is often thus, in the minor poets, that the tendencies of an age are most apparent. They are more fanatical than the great in their support of doctrines and fashions, more lacking in that final sense of humour and proportion which prevents excess. The outstanding writers are first and foremost individuals and no movement can claim their entire allegiance and loyalty. They soon liberate themselves from influences and restraints, soon cease from being typical of their group, and finally, in their maturity, become themselves alone. The ardent 'groupists', when the wave of the movement has broken and subsided, are left stranded on the beaches with no motive power of their own to ride the next wave. The shores of literature are littered with these shattered wrecks which once sailed so proudly, but which a strong wind swept along in its fury and flung on to the rocks. Now their storm-tossed hulks only show clearly what was the fashion of a bygone age.

Petrus Borel, with his artificiality and craziness, had many admirable talents and qualities as an artist. He had a high regard for literature and was incapable of compromising with his artistic standards for the sake of gain. He also had a hatred of injustice and intolerance which became ridiculous only because he lacked judgment and a sense of proportion. His compassion for those who had failed had something in it of Baudelaire's, though it tended, at times, to become a kind of nostalgia for failure. He was incapable of adapting himself to material circumstances and life finally broke him.

It is not easy to paint an intimate and convincing psychological picture of Petrus Borel since obvious and easily accessible material does not exist. His friends and relations do not seem to have kept his letters, and odd ones only have come down to us which have appeared in reviews. That rich mine for the study of the nineteenth-century—the *Collection Spoehlberch de Lovenjoul*, preserved in the Library of the French Academy at Chantilly—has no letters or documents dealing with Petrus Borel, save one unpublished letter from his widow addressed to Théophile Gautier to enlist his patronage in support of her son with the object of obtaining for him a free place at the Lycée of Algiers. This letter[1] permits us to correct the false statements made by all previous biographers of Petrus Borel concerning the birth of this child. The only large collection of his letters which has been discovered are those written to his superiors, in the last phase of his life, when he was Inspector of Colonisation in Algeria, letters dealing only with his official duties. These letters, with the answers to them and other relative documents, are preserved in the *Archives Nationales* in Paris,[2] and they give a complete picture of his career in North Africa. It is a pity that similar records do not exist for his earlier and more important period. Four unpublished letters from this period are however mentioned in Appendix III.

We know little of Petrus Borel's family life and nothing of his emotional life. If it is true, as Audin claims,[3] that the woman who became his mother-in-law, Antoinette Claye, had formerly been his mistress, we learn nothing about this fact from his contemporaries. Those who have written of him have always done so as if they had never known him intimately—perhaps no one ever did succeed in drawing near to him. The material for a study of his career is to be found chiefly in the memoirs of the time where he passes flamboyantly as a striking figure in fancy dress. The first biography of the poet, written by Jules Claretie, with the aid of the poet's brother, André Borel d'Hauterive, and published within six years of his death, is fantastic and untrue. The only complete study hitherto is the one by the late Aristide Marie which, in spite of its limitations and errors of fact, gives, up to date, the fairest and truest picture of the poet, but his position amongst his contemporaries is not sufficiently stressed, nor his importance for his successors. His Algerian career has been related by the present author.[4]

The present monograph is intended to be not merely a portrait of Petrus Borel himself but of his age as well; it is deliberately digressive, and there is much in it which does not concern the poet alone. Its intention is to paint a picture of the unsettled five or six years which followed the July Revolution, that Limbo which lies between the Romantic and Art for Art's Sake movements, when the seeds of much that is characteristic of later poetry were sown. It was a time of revolt against all conventions, in the arts, in politics, in manners and morals, and in it we find much of what is usually called Baudelairean. This monograph is also intended to be the first link in a chain which binds together a series of poets too often neglected in histories of French literature—Borel, Baudelaire, Corbière, Lautréamont, Rimbaud, Laforgue and Apollinaire. The *Bouzingos* of the eighteen-thirties were already the *Poètes Maudits* of the eighteen-eighties.

Except where otherwise stated, the edition of the works of Petrus Borel referred to is always that of *Les Forces Françaises*; it does not however contain his entire works.

Oxford, *May* 1953

Part One

THE MELTING POT

Chapter I

THE EARLY YEARS

T he family history of Petrus Borel, as told by his first
biographer, Jules Claretie, rivals in extravagance the
adventures of his own heroes. According to this
account his father was a nobleman from the Province
of Dauphiné, an ardent royalist, who played the part of a local
'Chouan' during the Revolution. Claretie declares that he swept
down with his men from his estates in the mountains to offer his
support to Virieu and to General de Précy in their stand against
the forces of the Revolution. Little by little however these royal-
ists were forced to yield and were driven back on to the heights of
Ferrières where they were finally crushed and captured by the
republican troops during the cruel reprisals of Fouché and Collot
d'Herbois. Borel d'Hauterive, the father of Petrus—so Claretie
says—escaped the guillotine through the devotion of an old family
servant who helped him to flee to Switzerland. Then followed the
Reign of Terror in Lyons during which scores of noblemen were
executed and the lands and goods of those who had fled across the
frontier were confiscated. Borel d'Hauterive, who had departed
without resources, lived, according to Claretie, in great poverty
abroad until the émigrés returned to France after the end of the
wars. Then he too went back, as poor as he had left, and settled
in Lyons to earn his living as best he could. He married and produced fourteen children. Later he migrated to Paris where he
opened a shop to provide for his numerous progeny.

This romantic legend is almost wholly untrue. Not that Claretie
is to blame since he obtained his material from the brother of the

poet, André Borel d'Hauterive. André Borel, like many another commoner in the democratic nineteenth century, was anxious to prove himself of noble extraction. Most of the Romantic writers tried to claim relationship with families who had borne noble titles and owned rich lands before the former were annulled and the latter confiscated during the Revolution. Those who could not honestly lay claim to such relationships had no scruples about inventing them. Witness Victor Hugo's attempts at proving that he was descended from the ancient and noble family of Hugo with whom he had no connection save similarity of name.

André Borel was passionately interested in heraldry and genea-logical research and, during the course of his studies, he dis-covered that a branch of the family of Hauterive had once borne the name of Borel. Near Grenoble there stood the Castle of Hauterive which came into possession of a Dauphin who pre-sented it in 1321 to Geoffroy de Clermont—a member of the younger branch of the family of Clermont Tonnerre. A couple of centuries later it was sold to a certain Amien Borel. On dis-covering this interesting fact André Borel began to investigate the history of Borels of Hauterive. He eventually produced a full and detailed account of the fortunes of the various members of this family, complete with copies of birth certificates and marriage contracts, with a description of their coat of arms. All this material he collected with the meticulous care of a scholar, but nowhere does he state his grounds for linking his own family with that of the historical Borel d'Hauterive. Having published this work of erudition André Borel had no scruples about adopting the name and the coat of arms of Hauterive for himself and his descendants. Petrus however, who was more scrupulous and—in his early years at all events—more genuinely democratic, refused, for the greater part of his life, to be party to this deception and continued to sign himself plain Borel. In the Preface to his first work he voices disgust of the pretentions to nobility of the Romantic poets. It was only very much later, when he had become a Civil Servant, and thought that the title might be of use to him in his profession, that he followed the example of his brother and adopted the suffix 'Hauterive'.

The truth about the Borel family is vastly different from this highly coloured romance. There was nothing of the legendary nobleman about the father of Petrus. He was a simple and unpretentious ironmonger and there is no justification whatsoever for linking his name with that of Borel d'Hauterive. He was born in 1765, the son of a small shopkeeper who married a certain Marguerite Garnaud; both the parents died when their son was still a child and he was brought up by his maternal uncle who owned an ironmonger's shop in Lyons. When he grew up he entered his uncle's business and eventually married his cousin, called Marguerite after her dead aunt. We know nothing of her family but there would seem to have been some culture and artistic talent on her side—one relative was an architect. Yet André Borel tells us nothing about her although it is probably from her that he and his brothers inherited their artistic and intellectual talents. After his marriage her husband opened an ironmonger's shop of his own in the Rue des Quatre Chapeaux which, then as now, was a street of small and rather mean shops. There, between 1791 and 1812, fourteen children were born of whom Petrus, born in 1809, was the twelfth.

The revolution certainly affected the fortunes of the family. Borel, in common with most of the middle class at Lyons, had royalist sympathies but there is no evidence that he was seriously implicated in the resistance of General Précy which led to the despatch of Fouché and Collot d'Herbois to Lyons in October 1793 and to the Terror there which lasted from the beginning of December until the following April, and during which it is alleged that over fifteen hundred executions took place. He cannot have been very seriously involved since his sole punishment was a fine of five hundred francs. He paid his fine and, as soon as the Reign of Terror was over, settled down to his ironmongering and breeding of children, piling up, franc by franc, sufficient capital to give them a good start in life. He believed in education and was able to secure for his many sons the best training available at that time.

The little we know of Petrus Borel's early life we learn from the autobiographical introduction to *Champavert*—we do not know whether it is all true but it has the ring of verisimilitude. As a child he would seem, from this account, to have been obstinate, self-willed and undisciplined and to have been proud of these characteristics as a sign of independence and strength of personality. It is however possible to see in them evidence of instability of character rather than independence, that instability which was later to lead to his ruin. He says that, as a boy, he was happy only in the country at Grand-Villars where his father possessed a cottage; there he was allowed to run wild, free from all restraint, to wander alone amongst the mountains, and this life made him grow in strength and toughness.

From an early poem, *Larme à mon Frère Benoni*, we gather that one of the tenderest emotions of his childhood was the love he felt towards an older brother who died young after a delicate childhood.

When his three youngest sons reached an age to be educated, the father, now getting on in years, sold his business in Lyons and retired to Paris to live on his accumulated savings, and to devote his remaining years to the training of his young boys. This would seem to be evidence of some means and prosperity.

Petrus was first sent as a pupil to the *Petit Séminaire Sainte Elizabeth*, but later an old friend of the family obtained for him a free place at the *Petit Séminaire Saint Roch*. No official records exist of his life at school, but according to his own account the sole result of his education in these religious institutions was to foster in him violent atheism and anti-clericalism. 'No man is a hero to his valet,' he wrote in *Champavert*[1] 'and no God is a God to those who serve the Church.' If *Champavert* is not exaggerated he must indeed have been a very difficult pupil since he became aware, at an early age, of the ignorance and intolerance of his teachers, and he did not hide his scorn or his contempt. He showed the same arrogance towards them that Baudelaire was to show towards his own teachers at the *Lycée Louis le Grand*.

Even as a schoolboy Petrus Borel had already acquired that passion for collecting scraps of learning which was later to develop into vain erudition and pedantry. He relates how, at school, he lived surrounded by learned tomes, by the works of old grammarians, by old dictionaries, books which he claimed made his

masters so ashamed of their ignorance that they would confiscate
them as soon as they saw them. Later he was to show the same
interest in linguistics, in curious and rare words, in old-fashioned
turns of phrase, in antiquated forms of spelling. This erudition
was however frequently faulty and ill-applied.

The enforced communal existence of the boarding-school,
which he unwillingly endured, fostered in him a passion for
solitude. It was probably at this time that he became confirmed in
his maladjustment to his surroundings. He never learned in his
adult life to adjust himself to his life, whatever it might be. In his
boyhood he was known amongst his school-fellows for his moods
of black melancholy and for his frequent outbursts of tears. He
could weep, he said, for several hours without pause.

As a boy his chief talent seems to have been for drawing. His
father, seeing that he was not happy at school, removed him and
apprenticed him to an architect called Antoine Garnaud, a relative
of his wife, but this did not please Petrus Borel any better than
school life.

'Yesterday my father said to me,' he wrote in *Champavert*[2] 'you
are a big boy now and everyone must have a profession—this was
November 1823 and I was barely fourteen—I shall give you a
master who will treat you well. You will be trained for a profession which should please you since you are for ever and always
scribbling on the walls, and since you are so good at drawing
poplars and soldiers. You will be trained for a good profession.
I did not then know what that meant. I followed my father and he
sold me into slavery for two years.'

The following January he wrote, after he had been for three
months under his master, 'So this is what a profession means, a
master, an apprentice? I do not understand it at all, but I'm sad
and I meditate on life which seems to me all too short. In our
passage through this world why must we have so many cares? So
much heart-breaking labour? What is the good of it all?' He could
not endure the thought of settling down and taking a profession
before he had had time to enjoy life. 'I laugh when I think of a
man settling down,' he cried. 'Settling down forsooth! What does
a man need in life? Only a bearskin and a little food! When I

used to dream of my life it certainly wasn't of such a life that I dreamed. Oh my father! The life I dreamed of was that of a camel-driver in the desert, or that of an Andalusian muleteer!'

The unhappiness and sense of frustration of his life was increased because he did not approve of the teaching of his master which he considered archaic and unimaginative. In 1823 Garnaud was still professing the classical style of architecture, whilst Borel, nurtured on the novels of Walter Scott, dreamed only of mediaeval castles. Finally he left his master to finish his training with a more advanced teacher called Boulard and, after five years of apprenticeship, set up his own office in 1829 at the age of twenty. He had naturally few commissions at first since he was young and unknown, and he lived in great poverty, often on the charity of a fellow architect called Louis Clopet, to whom he dedicated, in gratitude, the Prologue of his first book *Les Rhapsodies.*

Eventually he obtained some contracts and he is said to have drawn up the plans for the circus on the Boulevard du Temple, and to have built several houses. These houses did not however satisfy the Building Society which had commissioned them, and doubts were expressed about their soundness, since Borel would never follow any plans—not even his own. Objections were still being raised while the fourth house was being built, so he pulled down what he had already constructed and tore up his contract.

During the years of his apprenticeship Borel had become more interested in literature than in architecture, and he had even composed some poems. Shortly after he was qualified an event occurred which changed the whole course of his life and made him abandon the profession for which he was trained. In 1829 he made the acquaintanceship of two young artists, the brothers, Eugène and Achille Devéria, and through them he came into contact with the main writers of the Romantic Movement.

Chapter 2

LE PETIT CÉNACLE

———————————

Friendship with the Devéria brothers had a decisive effect on Petrus Borel's career. It gave him belief in himself, confidence in his poetic talent and courage to persevere in his literary ambitions. He now realised that, in his architectural studies, he had been following a path unsuited to him, and that his proper medium of expression was poetry. Now he felt compelled to play his part in the war to the death which was being waged between rising Romanticism and decaying Classicism.

The years from 1827 to 1830 were critical and vital years in the history of French poetry. This was the militant phase of the Romantic revolution—as significant a period as that of the *Pléiade* in the sixteenth century—when the young writers were fighting, no longer in the haphazard manner of Lamartine, but an organised battle against the classical tradition, in order to establish their own. It was verily a second Renaissance and Hugo's *Préface de Cromwell* of 1827 became the manifesto of the young movement, a new *Défense et Illustration de la Langue Française*. The struggle was finally won at the *Bataille d'Hernani* in February 1830, but there had been preliminary skirmishes in 1829 with Vigny's *Othello* and Dumas' *Henri III et sa Cour*. It is true that Vigny's play was little more than a free adaptation of Shakespeare's, but its production was hailed, nevertheless, as an important victory for the Romantic Movement, a non-classical play produced in the stronghold of Classicism, the Comédie Française. Dumas' play, performed shortly afterwards, in the same theatre, was more significant, possessing as it did all the violence which the public had enjoyed in the melodrama of Pixérécourt. The play created a sensation with high society as well as with the masses, for Dumas had managed to secure the patronage of the Duke of Orleans who was destined to become King the following year and who was already, in 1829, the centre of much intrigue.

Later, in the autumn, it was rumoured that Victor Hugo was planning an important 'coup' for his production of *Hernani* the following year. It was expected that this would be something sensational since it was becoming increasingly evident that he was destined, in the immediate future, to become the leader of the new poets. Lamartine was too much of a dreamer, and moreover posed as being a gifted amateur rather than a professional writer. Vigny was too distant, too proud and seemingly too indifferent to ordinary humanity ever to attract a following. But Hugo had all the fire, the self-confidence, and also the absence of self-criticism, invaluable for a successful leader of men. The public now expected much from him and from the play which was announced for 1830.

Hugo, for his part, was very anxious to win a victory which would be spectacular and evident, and especially to outdistance Dumas' triumph. He determined to enlist the help of the followers whom he had collected amongst the youngest generation of writers, or would-be writers, and it was then that he turned to Petrus Borel whom he had already singled out for notice at the meetings of the *Cénacle* at Nodier's Sunday evenings.

Petrus Borel was at this time almost twenty-one and he had been living an adult and professional life for more than six years so that he felt much older and more experienced than the youths of his own age, barely out of school, whom he met at the studio of the Devéria brothers. He soon took the lead amongst the ten or twelve artists and poets whom he banded together to fight against Classicism. This group called itself 'Le Petit Cénacle' to distinguish themselves from the more famous elder *Cénacle* which met in Nodier's rooms. They prided themselves on their advanced revolutionary and republican ideals—in literature and in politics —on their hatred of convention, of the bourgeoisie and of everything classical. They all affected a mediaeval or early Renaissance pose, and to distinguish themselves from others altered their names to give them a mediaeval or exotic flavour. Thus Jean Dusseigneur became Jehan du Seigneur and Louis Bertrand, Aloysius Bertrand. Because they admired everything English—particularly Walter Scott—Auguste Maquet changed his name to Augustus MacKeat. Sometimes the modification was merely eccentric and thus Théophile Dondey altered his name, by anagram, to Philothée O'Neddy. Borel did not need to change his name for he had been christened 'Joseph Petrus'.

The members of 'Le Petit Cénacle' were as eccentric in their manners and dress as in their choice of names. Gautier, in his *Histoire du Romantisme*, has given us a picture of most of these young men. There was Jehan du Seigneur who brushed his hair up from two side partings into a high peak rising above his forehead, to simulate—says Gautier—the flame of genius. In place of a waistcoat he wore a black velvet doublet fitting tightly to his figure and laced up the back; over this a loose jacket with wide velvet revers and flowing black tie. He showed no trace of white, not even a collar. There was Eugène Devéria, famous even then for his picture *La Naissance d'Henri IV*, who was a magnificent figure dressed like a Spanish grandee. There were Ourlioff in his Cossack boots; Bouchardy in his bright-blue frock coat, with the gold buttons, like that worn by an Indian Maharajah; the two brothers, one nicknamed 'Le Gothic' and the other 'Le Christ', in their sweeping light-blue cloaks lined with pale pink, and fastened by pearl buttons as large as five shilling pieces; there was Célestin Nanteuil, one of the youngest, looking like an archangel who had stepped down from a mediaeval stained-glass window, who illustrated many of the exquisite editions of the poets of his generation, which are now highly prized by connoisseurs. There was Philothée O'Neddy of whom there will be more later. Finally there were—best known today—Gérard de Nerval and Théophile Gautier. The former, although barely twenty-one, had already received recognition for his translation of *Faust* which had found favour with Goethe himself, who had said, 'I have never understood myself so well as when I read your translation.'[1] Eckermann reports that he added 'I do not care for reading my *Faust* in

27

German any more but in this French translation it seems to me fresh, new and spirited'.[2] Gautier, at nineteen, was famous for nothing save his exuberant spirits and his flowing locks. The following year, at the *Bataille d'Hernani*, he was to reach notoriety on the score of his red velvet doublet—not waistcoat as is usually stated—and his pale green trousers with the black velvet stripe running down the side seams.

Amongst the members of the *Petit Cénacle* there was undoubtedly one who had supreme prestige, and that was Petrus Borel. He was, says Gautier,[3] the living incarnation of the spirit of poetry, not an ordinary mortal. At this time he looked as if he had stepped down from a Spanish picture and it would have been easy to imagine him slinking mysteriously through the streets of Seville, in his cloak 'couleur de muraille'. He had a haughty condescending courtesy which made him different from his contemporaries for, although a rebel, he was not rough or uncouth. It was this aristocratic quality which was to appeal to Baudelaire when he met him fifteen years later. His exaggerated stories and his paradoxes were received with the same open-mouthed amazement as were Baudelaire's later. The reputation which he enjoyed, probably undeserved, of indulging in passionate and exotic love-affairs further enhanced his notoriety and the glamour of this legend. His face was serious in expression, far older than his years, of perfect regularity of feature; his skin was of a light-olive colour, faintly golden, like the patina on an old painting; his eyes were bright but at the same time weighted with melancholy, hooded like the eyes of a hawk. His mouth was a brilliant red,—like an exotic flower beneath his moustache, Gautier describes it, and it possessed the mobility of the mouth of an oriental. But his most striking feature was his dark-brown beard, a silky beard faintly perfumed, that framed his face and gave him the appearance of a Sultan from the *Arabian Nights*. At that time, says Gautier, there were only two beards in the whole of Paris, that of Devéria and that of Borel, but Borel's was the finer, a full beard, an imperial beard, the beard of a leader.

At this time Petrus Borel used to wear a red waistcoat—the colour of Polish blood, he said—and a wide-brimmed hat with a bunch of motley ribbons flowing down to his waist behind. Later he was to dress more soberly in unrelieved black.

He used to affect in his speech a strange and paradoxical manner —the kind of manner adopted later by Baudelaire—and no one ever knew whether he meant seriously the outrageous things that he used to say. Like Baudelaire he was a brilliant talker and in 1829 he used still to enjoy society and had not yet become the lycan-thrope baying at the moon. In those days he could have posed for the perfect Byronic hero, 'l'homme fatal', proud of his good looks, arrogant in his behaviour, striding along, the centre of a host of admiring young men, with his long black cloak thrown over his shoulder, trailing his shadow behind him, as Gautier says, and woe betide the man who dared to tread on it.

At this time it used to be said that when his poems appeared, Victor Hugo would need to look to his laurels—Borel was only twenty then and had not yet published anything.

Later, when Petrus Borel had fallen from public favour, and when his former companions marvelled at the memory of his ascendancy, there were some who questioned his former supre-macy. Philothée O'Neddy, writing in 1862—Borel was then only three years dead—asserted that it was false to say that he had been the leader; that, on the contrary, Gautier and Gérard de Nerval had possessed equal prestige. By this time O'Neddy's memory must have grown dim with the passing of the years, for it was only at the very end of the thirties that Gautier's and Nerval's fame outstripped that of Borel. Gautier himself wrote,[4] 'There is in every age one powerful individuality round whom the others gravitate, like planets round their sun. Petrus Borel was that sun and none of us tried to resist the force of his attraction. As soon as one had entered his path one revolved happily round him as if following a law of nature.'

There can be no doubt that it was he who was the leader of the younger generation and it was to him, not to Gautier or Gérard de Nerval, that Victor Hugo turned, at the end of 1829, when he sought help to make the first night of *Hernani* a success which should make that of Dumas' *Henri III et sa Cour* pale into in-significance.

Chapter 3

LA BATAILLE D'HERNANI

T he Battle of *Hernani* was planned, with all the mystery of a Renaissance conspiracy, in Hugo's house in the Rue Notre Dame des Champs which had become the G.H.Q. of militant Romanticism. Borel and his followers could be seen creeping into the house late at night, looking as if they too, like Hernani himself, were 'chargés d'un mandat d'anathème'. They would slink along, in the shadow of the walls, their dark sombreros pulled down over their eyes, and their long cloaks slung over their shoulders, hiding in doorways if they heard anyone approaching. It was if they were in fact followers of a bandit chief, as if there were a price on their collective head. None of them was more than twenty-one, and the preparations for the battle had for them the exciting mystery of a game of childhood, but with the added reality of grown-up life, with real accessories instead of toys.

The 'claque' was an important feature of theatrical life in the nineteenth century, a by-product of the theatre, like the refreshments and the programmes, from which good profits could be earned. Each theatre had its corporation of 'claqueurs' under a leader, who received payment from the management and also collected fees from the actors and from the authors. If a rich patron wished to secure the success of a young actress in whom he was interested, he used, at first, to provide her with a luxurious version of the services of the 'claque', instead of jewels. Véron, the literary doctor, the founder of the *Revue de Paris*, was, in the thirties, the director of the Opera and, in his *Memoirs*,[1] describes the organisation of his 'claque'; it was probably the same in most theatres. He says that the leader made a good forty thousand francs a year from his employment, and most of this was made from the first nights of new plays. This leader was proud of his work and used frequently to boast, 'Quel beau succès j'ai obtenu.' He used to be invited to the rehearsals so that he should know the play beforehand and carefully plan his campaign. For a First Night he was granted a hundred free tickets in various parts of the house and he used to place his army in good strategic positions. No account of the Battle of *Hernani* has explained how Hugo managed to dispense with the services of the official 'claque'. He himself declared that he would have none of it because its members were too vitiated by applauding classical plays to appreciate anything new, and moreover he did not like applause which was bought, and that he would invite his own friends who would be genuinely moved to clap. Perhaps he could not afford the high fees of the corporation, or perhaps he had quarrelled with the leader. It is possible that some of the opposition at his First Night came from a counter 'claque' of professionals. Hugo was not a simple amateur, he was a century ahead of his time in his understanding of the value of publicity, and he would have had nothing to learn today from twentieth-century methods. He himself carefully coached his own private 'claque' and this took longer than the actual writing of the play itself which had taken him a bare three weeks. Petrus Borel had collected under his orders a band of a hundred students from the Latin Quarter whom he drilled in the passages where they were to cheer and they were to boo and to silence, with physical force if necessary, any opposition. To make the conspiracy more mysterious, instead of being given ordinary passes—that would have been too unromantic—they were issued with blood-red tickets on which was inscribed in bold black letters the Spanish word for 'iron', '*hierro*'.

The planning of the Battle distracted Hugo's mind from the difficulties he was encountering in the production of the play itself. Some of the subscribers of the Comédie Française had already protested to the Government about the nature of the plays now being produced in the State theatre by the progressive director,

Baron Taylor—melodramas like Dumas' *Henri III et sa Cour*—
and they said that if this were allowed to continue it would mean
the end of French drama. Charles X was also very much opposed
to the Romantic writers who were mostly liberals and in favour of
a change of régime. Hugo's first play, *Marion Delorme*, which was
to have been produced in 1829, had been banned because the King
considered that an unflattering portrait of his ancestor, Louis
XIII, had been drawn. Then the leading actors—the 'sociétaires'
of the Comédie Française—people of great importance in the
management of the theatre, were annoyed because the play had
been accepted by the Baron without previous consultation with
them, and they determined to make the unfortunate author suffer
because they had been slighted. Mademoiselle Mars, the leading
lady, was a protégée of the King and she agreed with him in con-
demning these upstart writers who had risen without patronage,
these writers with no traditions. In spite of the personal success
she had won in the part of the Duchesse de Guise in *Henri III et sa
Cour* she deplored the changes which were taking place in the
theatre under the influence of the new school. Dumas himself had
said that her pleasure in his play had in it all the 'réstrictions
mentales de la femme violée'.

The rehearsals of *Hernani* were difficult from the first and Hugo
had to fight every inch of the way.[2] He had none of the bonhomie
and good temper of Dumas who was bluff and hearty, shouted
loudly and gave as good as he received. Hugo, on the contrary,
was pompous and priggish, with a high idea of his own importance and dignity, and he was always icily polite. Circumstances
also did not favour him. The winter of 1829 to 1830 was one of
the coldest on record, and the Seine was frozen over from the
middle of December until the end of February. The actors shivered
with the cold and hurried through their parts to get back to the
stove. This impeded the rehearsals, made tempers short, and
developed animosities. From the first Hugo antagonised Mademoiselle Mars and she took it upon herself to humiliate him and
teach him his place. For her the rehearsals turned into a comic act,
in which she bear-baited the unfortunate author in front of an
admiring audience of sycophantic fellow-actors and stage-hands.

The members of the cast were glad of this comic relief in the weary task of rehearsing in the bitter cold.

Every day, just as the rehearsal was beginning, she would say to whichever actor was on the stage with her: 'One moment Monsieur Firmin, please,' or 'one moment Monsieur Johanney, please.' as the case might be, 'I want to say a word to the author.' Then, while everyone else was silent, she would go to the front of the stage and, shielding her eyes from the glare of the footlights, would peer down into the dark well of the theatre, pretending to be looking for Victor Hugo, though she knew perfectly well that he was always in his usual place right in the front row. She would then call in a loud voice which re-echoed through the empty auditorium: 'Is Monsieur Hugo in the theatre? Will someone find Monsieur Hugo for me!'

'I'm here, Madame,' he would answer each day, rising from his seat and speaking with icy politeness as he tried to keep his temper.

'Very good!' she would answer, 'And must I *really* say that line, Monsieur Hugo?'

'Which line, Madame?'

'Vous êtes, mon lion, superbe et généreux!'

Suppressed titters from those who were waiting.

'Yes, Madame,' he answered coldly, 'you must say it since it is in the text. Hernani says to you:

> *Hélas j'aime pourtant d'une amour bien profonde!*
> *Ne pleure pas . . . Mourons plutôt! Que n'ai-je un monde,*
> *Je te le donnerais! Je suis bien malheureux!*

Then you answer: "Vous êtes, mon lion, superbe et généreux!" '

Mademoiselle Mars would then go back to her place on the stage, raising her eyes to Heaven with an air of mock resignation and as if to call all the others to witness of her patience, but she stopped half-way and returned to the foot-lights to say: 'And do you really think that that is a good line, Monsieur Hugo?'

'Which line?' he would reply, as if in ignorance.

'Vous êtes, mon lion, superbe et généreux!'

'I wrote it Madame' he answered, pale with anger, 'and so I must think it good.'

'But it seems to me a very funny thing to call respectable Monsieur Firmin, a lion.'

'You must remember, Madame', he answered calmly, 'that he is not Monsieur Firmin in the play, and that you are not Mademoiselle Mars.'

'Well! since you cling to your "lion", let's say no more about it. After all I'm here to say what is in the text and what do I care anyway! It's all one to me, Mon Dieu! Come on Firmin, let's get on with it. "Vous êtes, mon lion, superbe et généreux!" '

The rehearsals would continue, but the following day, when she reached the same place, she would pause again and pretend that she did not remember what had been decided the previous day. As before she stopped the rehearsal, went to the front of the stage and called, as before, 'Monsieur Hugo!'

'I'm here, Madame.'

'I'm very glad that you're here! Have you thought about that little matter we were discussing yesterday?'

'Which little matter, Madame?'

'The question of the line, "Vous êtes, mon lion, superbe et généreux!" '

This line had now become, for the rest of the cast and the stagehands, a humorous tag. Hugo answered that he had thought nothing and that the line must stand.

'But don't you think it a dangerous line, Monsieur Hugo?' she asked. 'Why dangerous, Madame?'

'I call dangerous any line which runs the risk of provoking laughter, and being hissed.'

There must be many who sympathise with Mademoiselle Mars in her condemnation of this supremely foolish line. On the first night it is alleged that she did not in fact say it, but substituted 'Vous êtes, mon Seigneur, superbe et généreux!' By that time however no one was listening to the words actually spoken on the stage and it would not have mattered what she had said. In any case Hugo must, at the end, have given way on this point for in the first published edition of *Hernani*, the emendation is to be found.

In another scene she was supposed to stand motionless as a

statue and to remain silent spectator of a scene which took place
between Don Carlos and Ruy Gomez. She was to take no part in
the scene until the King was about to arrest Ruy Gomez, then she
had to fling herself between them and cry: 'Roi Carlos, vous êtes
un mauvais roi!' The long silence and immobility were very trying
to Mademoiselle Mars and she did not know what to do during
the interminable speeches of the other actors in which she took
no part. One day she interrupted the rehearsal in her usual manner
and said: 'Are you there, Monsieur Hugo?'

'Yes, Madame!'

'I should be grateful if you would oblige me!'

'Willingly, Madame!'

'Then will you please tell me what I'm supposed to be doing in
this scene!'

'In which scene, Madame?'

'In the scene where Monsieur Michelot and Monsieur Johanney
are chatting away together!'

'You are supposed to be listening, Madame.'

'Ah! I see, listening! But it seems to me that I listen a little too
long! Couldn't you shorten it a bit?'

'No, Madame, impossible!'

'Or else let me play some part in it?'

'But you are playing a part in it, Madame, by your mere
presence. They are discussing the man you love, deciding the
question of his life or death. It seems to that the situation is
sufficiently powerful for you to wait silently until the end!'

'But all the same I think it is a bit long.'

'I don't consider it so!'

'All right then! Don't let's mention it any more! But the
audience will certainly think, "what on earth is Mademoiselle
Mars doing there, with her hand glued to her bosom? What is the
point of giving her a part if she is to be kept standing there with a
veil over her face, without speaking a single word for a whole
act?"'

'No, Madame, the public won't think that at all! It will only
think that it isn't Mademoiselle Mars who is standing there, but
Dona Sol; that beneath her hand her heart is beating; that beneath

that veil it is not the face of Mademoiselle Mars but that of Dona
Sol, which grows red with hope or pale with fear; that during that
silence—not of Mademoiselle Mars but of Dona Sol, the lover of
Hernani—the storm is gathering in her heart, which will break
out in the words: "Roi Carlos, vous êtes un mauvais roi!" and
believe me, Madame, that will satisfy the public!'

'Well! that's only your opinion! But I don't know why I trouble
my head about all that! If they hiss the scene it won't be me they'll
be hissing, for I shan't be saying a word! Come on Michelot, come
on Johanney, let's get on with it!'

The following day she began again at the same place her usual
comedy of calling Hugo and then said to him: 'Well! Monsieur
Hugo, and have you thought of anything for me to say?'

'Where, Madame?'

'You know well, in the famous scene where these two gentlemen spout a hundred and fifty lines while I stare at them in
silence!'

'Firstly, Madame, the scene hasn't a hundred and fifty lines, but
only seventy-six, for I've counted them! Secondly I didn't promise
to find anything for you to say. On the contrary, I tried to prove
to you that your silence, your immobility, out of which you
suddenly burst, were the real beauty of the scene!'

'And so you're determined that I'm to say nothing?'

'Yes! Madame, I'm determined!'

'Well! I don't care! I'll only go to the back of the stage and let
these gentlemen get on with their business together!'

'You'll go to the back of the stage if you like, but, as their
business is also your business, you'll only make nonsense of the
scene!'

And thus the rehearsals continued with never-ending inter-
ruptions. In the end Hugo lost his temper and threatened to give
the part of Dona Sol to someone else. This was an unparalleled
insult to a 'sociétaire' of the Comédie Française and only with the
utmost difficulty were she and the rest of the cast pacified and
prevailed upon not to resign their parts.

Mademoiselle Mars, in spite of their objections to the play, was
a genuine and scrupulous actor and she could not help giving of

her best at the actual performances. Michelot, on the contrary, used to indicate, by the tone of his voice, which passages he considered ludicrous, and he invited the mockery of the audience.

The rehearsals finally came to an end, and the First Night arrived.[3]

The management of the theatre had reserved for Hugo's 'claque' the orchestra pit, the Second Circle and all but fifty places in the Pit. The leader of the official 'claque' usually got to the theatre early in order to place his men and to give them his final instructions. Borel and his followers were to be allowed into the theatre at three o'clock in the afternoon—whether they requested this early hour, or whether they were obliged to accept it, is not known. They were told to present themselves at one of the principal entrances, but it would have been wiser if they had been admitted, as the 'claque' usually was, through a side door into one of the passages at the back of the theatre. To make a greater show they arrived at the theatre at one o'clock and were kept waiting for two whole hours in the street—a main thoroughfare—and all who passed saw an extraordinary crowd dressed in every kind of fancy-dress, some with Spanish cloaks, some in Robespierre waistcoats, some in mediaeval tunics, one with a Henri III hat and Gautier in his famous scarlet doublet. Many of the young men were unwashed and they looked a regular pack of ragamuffins. The respectable people stopped with amazement and disapproval at this motley gathering and soon a crowd collected to watch them while they retaliated by making grimaces. Then the crowd began to attack them, seizing as weapons anything they could find—sticks, stones and garbage from the gutters—and began to pelt them with them. Balzac received a cabbage stalk full in the face. Still the doors of the theatre did not open. The Romantics wished to retaliate but Petrus Borel explained to them that this would make the police intervene and they would not be able to attend the performance—perhaps that indeed was what the opponents had wanted—and they kept a superhuman restraint on themselves.

Finally the doors opened and the 'claque' went to the places reserved for them. They were then locked into the theatre and debarred from the cloak-rooms for four hours until the play began, with results which can be imagined. Soon they were in total darkness for they were given no lights, and evening falls early in February. They had to find some way of passing the weary hours of waiting. They played round games, sang obscene songs, imitated wild animals—in fact behaved as students do the whole world over. They had brought their evening meal with them, and it consisted of strong-smelling food—garlic, onion, sausages, and many bottles of wine.

After three hours the lights began to appear, one by one. The chandelier descended and lit up. Baudelaire once said 'What I have always thought most beautiful in the theatre—in my childhood and still nowadays—is the chandelier'. Certainly no one ever hailed its descent with more eagerness than did Borel and his young companions that night of *Hernani*. Next the 'Early Doors' began to pour into the gallery and the pit at half past six. More lights burst out along the rim of the boxes and circles—an edging of sparkling jewels. Finally the Grand Circle, the Boxes and the Stalls filled with beautiful young women looking like flowers in their gay and delicately coloured frocks. As each of them moved to the front of the box the young Romantics clapped and cheered. Women were not participants in this battle to the death, and a beautiful girl was beyond all strife. The men in the stalls and in the Grand Circle all seemed elderly, with bald pates and heavy paunches. They were probably supporters of the classicists for they made a pretence of holding their noses and talked of the Barbarians desecrating the temple of Melpomene.

When Hugo arrived at the theatre the door-keeper said to him: 'Monsieur Hugo your play will be a flop, and it's your friends who will have killed it!' Mademoiselle Mars summoned him to her dressing-room and said to him: 'Well! you've a nice lot of friends, I must say! Do you know what they've done?' Then, as he did not answer, she went on: 'I've played before to all sorts of different publics before this one, but I'll owe it to you to play before such a one!'

Hugo then went on to the stage and peered through the little spy-hole in the curtain into the auditorium. The theatre was com-

THÉOPHILE GAUTIER
at the *Bataille d'Hernani*
From a self portrait

pletely full! All smart society was there, and everyone of importance had bought tickets when these could still be obtained, but he
himself had received requests from those who had not succeeded
in getting any at the box-offices, demands from Mérimée, Constant and others—even from Thiers.

Finally the three traditional knocks sounded. The curtain rose,
revealing a sixteenth-century bedroom lit by a lamp, in which an
elderly duenna was seated sewing. Then a tap sounded on the
secret door, and there followed the famous couplet in which the
'enjambement' occurred:

> *Serait-ce déjà lui? C'est bien à l'escalier*
> *Dérobé* . . .

At this the fight began and there was no further chance of hearing
a single line of the play. Every phrase was cheered or booed
according to the taste of the supporters or opponents. There were
outraged protests from the Classicists when the King asked, just
like any ordinary bourgeois: 'Est-il minuit?' To which the
plebeian answer came: 'Minuit bientôt!' Whereas the rules of
literary decorum would have demanded an elegant periphrasis
such as:

> *L'heure*
> *Atteindra bientôt sa dernière demeure.*

An unexpected diversion occurred when Charles V protests at
Ruy Gomez having allowed Dona Sol to depart with Hernani.
'Vieillard stupide il l'aime!' he cried. Then Monsieur Perzeval de
Grandmaison, an ardent supporter of the Classicists—but also
hard of hearing—thought that he heard, 'Vieil as de pique il
l'aime!' Although 'as de pique' literally means 'ace of spades', it
also means the 'Pope's nose' of a fowl, and it is an insult to apply
the epithet to anyone, intending to suggest that he is ugly and
misbegotten. Monsieur de Grandmaison thought that here was
one of the daring metaphors of the new school, of which they
were so proud, now cried out in indignation: 'Ma foi! that is going
too far!' 'What is going too far?' demanded young Lassailly[4]
truculently, who was an ardent supporter of the Romantics. Then
Monsieur de Grandmaison answered: 'Nothing will ever make me

believe that it is not going too far to call a respectable old man like Ruy Gomez, "vieil as de pique!" ' Lassailly insisted that this was one of the finest metaphors in the whole play and that, moreover, the author had a perfect right to use it since cards had been invented at the time of Charles V. 'Les cartes étaient inventées, Monsieur l'Académicien, si vous ne saviez pas cela, je vous l'apprends! Bravo pour le vieil as de pique!'[5]

So the battle raged, line after line. But traditional French courtesy was often lost in the heat of the fray. 'Madame, you are wrong to laugh,' said Monsieur de Saxe-Cobourg to his neighbour, during the scene of the portraits which Mademoiselle Mars had indeed feared might cause laughter. 'You are wrong to laugh, you're showing all your back teeth.'

The Battle of *Hernani* was on a Saturday night and on the following morning the notices began to appear. Except for the *Journal des Débats*, all were hostile. The articles did not confine themselves to artistic criticism, but Hugo was attacked on the score of his 'claque' and the disgraceful behaviour of Borel and his followers. They were said to have made of the theatre 'une caverne nauséabonde', to have sung obscene songs there, to have had orgies in it, and to have desecrated forever the Temple of dramatic art.

The fight continued for several performances but henceforth the 'claque' was admitted only a few moments before the curtain rose. Now there was mockery for the play itself and less fury for the cause. It must be admitted that the scoffers often had reason on their side.

The play however eventually triumphed over all its attackers. This marked the end of the battle between Classicism and Romanticism. Lamartine, when he saw the outcome of the fight, said 'these wretched words classic and romantic have fallen into the bottomless pit of 1830'. In February 1830 one stronghold of Classicism, La Comédie Française, had fallen to the new school, and later in the same year another was to open its gates also when Lamartine was elected a member of the French Academy.

1830 was the highest point of the Romantic struggle and the movement did not try to advance beyond the position it had gained at that time and settled down to consolidate its triumphs. By then it had become conservative and liable to criticism, and indeed was soon to be attacked even by some of its supporters on the night of *Hernani*.

As a result of the victory of *Hernani*, Hugo was left as unchallenged leader of Romanticism, but he now separated himself from his former friends and associates—especially from the rough young bohemians who had helped him in the fray—and he began now to take himself very seriously as the Master. He then moved away from the Rue Notre Dame de Champ, in the Latin Quarter, and settled in a richer house, in the Place Royale, which now houses the *Musée Victor Hugo*. Here the most glorious and most successful years of his career were spent, during the reign of Louis Philippe.

Chapter 4

THE JULY REVOLUTION

I t is not only in the literary field that revolt took place in
1830. In July occurred the political revolution which brought
the Bourbon dynasty to an end and inaugurated the bourgeois regime of Louis Philippe.

The country had been in a very disturbed state since the accession of Charles X in 1824. Louis XVIII, old and infirm after his
long years of exile, asked only for a quiet life and to be permitted
to die while still King of France. He achieved this ambition and
was in fact the last of France's rulers to die in office, for Charles X,
Louis Philippe and Napoleon III all died in exile.

Charles X was a very different person from his brother Louis
XVIII. He was younger and more bitter against the Revolution,
and more unforgiving for the execution of his brother and sister-
in-law—yet, as the Comte d'Artois, he had formerly supported
Beaumarchais, when Louis XVI had banned *Le Mariage de Figaro*.
He was determined, when he came to the throne, to clear away
the changes which still remained from the Revolution. He considered that his predecessor had been very remiss and lacking
in loyalty to his house, in accepting the new constitution. After
the end of the Napoleonic Wars, when the Allies had put Louis
XVIII on to the throne of France, the English, in the historic
manner of the English, insisted that certain liberties gained by the
Revolution should be preserved, but by 1824, again in their
historic manner, they had lost interest in the affairs of the conti-
nent and had withdrawn to the isolation of their island, leaving
Charles X to do what he wished. His years of exile had only

fostered in him the faults of his house, the vices which had led to the Revolution. He roused dissatisfaction, first by the mediaeval pomp of the Coronation, and next by increasing the power of the Church; he reintroduced the conception of the Divine Right of Kings and the practice of curing the King's Evil by the laying on of hands—he used to visit the hospitals for the purpose. From his accession unrest had been growing until, in 1827, at the elections, his party suffered a reverse which was followed by a moderate government under Martignac. In 1829, however, Polignac came to power. He had gone into exile with Charles X forty years before, had fought in the Royalist rising in La Vendée during the Revolution, and, in 1814, had refused to sign his allegiance to the Charter. No more unpopular man could have been chosen, at this moment of great dissatisfaction with the King, to lead the government, and all the other members of his party were equally unpopular. His aims were those of his royal Master—to restore completely all the privileges of the old régime and give more power to the Church. One of the greatest enemies of this reactionary movement was the Press and so Charles X determined to silence it. Matters, however, had changed very much since 1789 for there had arisen a strong and educated bourgeoisie amongst whom were many distinguished and progressive journalists. Now this aristocracy of intellect struggled for power with the aristocracy of birth. Amongst them was Thiers who had written a history of the Revolution, who believed in the Rights of Man and was determined to teach the people what were these rights. He was the editor of the *National* and, in January and February 1830, wrote in it a series of articles which discussed the benefits of a constitutional monarchy—he had Louis Duke of Orleans in mind, the son of Philippe Egalité who had voted for the execution of his cousin Louis XVI.

There was much poverty during the winter of 1829 to 1830—due partly to the very severe weather—and there was much unemployment which led to processions of workmen demanding work. Finally, in May, the Chamber passed a vote of no-confidence in Polignac and the King dissolved it. Elections were held in June and Polignac's party was defeated at the polls. Hopes then arose that there might be the possibility of a more progressive government. At that moment the King and Polignac planned their 'coup'. The Charter of 1815 had laid down that all power came from the Sovereign, and Article XIV gave him the power, in an emergency, to suspend the laws and to pass the legislation himself during the time of crisis. Charles X decided that such a time of crisis existed and determined to use his authority to quash the results of the election, and to appoint his own government. On July 25 the four *Ordinances* were signed. The first stipulated complete Crown control over the Press, the second dissolved the Chamber, the third altered the franchise to suit the King, and the fourth ordered elections for the following September.

When the *Ordinances* were made public on July 26 the country was appalled at the audacity of the King for, in spite of the rumours, no one had believed that he would really sign them. This act set fire to the powder magazine and the Revolution started.

There were two parties opposed to the King who were in favour of a Revolution. On the one hand there were those who wished to see a Republic established; on the other were those who wished to put the Duke of Orleans on the throne as a constitutional monarch. Most of the young intelligentsia were on the side of the Republicans, but the Orleanists had Thiers, Guizot Talleyrand, Lafayette, and all the financial interests; they had the solid bourgeoisie behind them but no soldiers. They contented themselves with drawing up plans and then waited quietly for events. It was the Republicans who fought in the streets, who manned the barricades and won the victory in the field. Then thousands of them, under Cavaignac, routed the royal armies. In these days Paris was a maze of narrow streets, and these were very helpful for guerilla warfare. No artillery could be brought up against them, and the insurgents used paving-stones, poured boiling water and threw furniture from their houses down on the troops who were helpless in the face of such attack. Fighting began on July 27 and lasted three days—'Les Trois Glorieuses' they were later called. On July 28 Charles X's soldiers were utterly defeated, and what was left of the armies went over to the rebels. On July 29 the Louvre was attacked and the Suisses, terrified of a repetition of the massacres of August 1792, fled in disorder. By the end of the day the tricolour flag floated over every public building in Paris.

When Charles X heard of the disaster he retired to Rambouillet and abdicated in favour of his grandson. This however availed him nothing for the boy king, the Regent and the whole government were all swept away. But, as so often happens, the winning insurgents were completely taken by surprise by the swiftness of their success, and they had no plans ready to meet such an emergency. Then the Orleanists stepped forward with their prepared schemes and got them accepted. The Duke put a bunch of tricolour ribbons in his hat and, holding the tricolour flag in his hand, marched to the Hôtel de Ville, where Thiers proposed him as King. He was at first greeted by cries of 'A bas les Bourbons!', then he appeared in the balcony with Lafayette at his side—this was a stroke of genius—and embraced him before the crowd. That carried the day, for Lafayette was the idol of the country because his participation in the American revolution had made of him, in the eyes of the mob, the champion of liberty. Seeing him with the Duke of Orleans, the crowd imagined that all must be well, and accepted the King they were offered. Thus Louis achieved what his father had never succeeded in doing in spite of all his efforts; he made himself King of the French.

All the members of the 'Petit Cénacle' were republican at heart, but they did not think it necessary to fight personally in the Revolution, as their younger brothers were to do in the Revolution of 1848 when Louis Ménard, Leconte De Lisle and Baudelaire, all took an active, if not very glorious, part in the fighting. The 'Petit Cénacle' considered that the function of its members was to devote their energies to art even whilst the battle raged round them. Bouchardy used to say: 'Our pens, our paint-brushes and our chisels were our sole arms, the great Masters our only Gods, and Art the flag we tried to defend.'[1]

Petrus Borel, unlike his friends was, on the contrary, most violently republican. In the Preface to his first published work, *Rhapsodies*, he wrote: 'If I talk of republicanism it is because that word represents for me the greatest amount of liberty which civilisation and society can provide. I need an enormous amount of liberty.' But when he saw what were the results of the Revolution which he had desired so ardently, and how the country had been cheated of the fruits of the victory it had won, then his spirit of chivalry was roused and the Spanish grandee in him could not bear to allow this interloper to profit from the blood of others. It is said that he tried to dash out and sacrifice his life on the barricades and in the fighting in the streets, to defend the republican cause, but that his father locked him up in the house. All that was left for him to do was to attack the new King in his writings. He was never to forgive Louis Philippe for what he considered his treachery to the country, and, in *Madame Putiphar*, published eight years later, whilst reviewing the exploits of those who, in his opinion, during the course of French history, had destroyed the country, he declared that there finally came one to put the finishing touches to the work of his predecessors and added: 'Then God, to complete the holocaust, will choose a tool from the very dynasty of that people and make him reign over them until they have expiated his recent heinous crimes and treachery, a man with claw-like hands,* having a nipper for sceptre; a gigantic lobster with no blood in its veins, but whose shell is the colour of spilt blood.'[2]

This portrait, more striking rhetorically than correct zoologically, is intended for Louis Philippe.

* *Mains crochues* in French means, as well as 'claw-like hands', 'rapacious and light-fingered'.

Part Two

THE AFTERMATH

Chapter I

SPLEEN

The Revolution of 1830 left behind it a sensation of disappointment and disillusionment, and those who had built high hopes on it were in a state of discouragement often bordering on despair. The suffering, the sacrifice and the bloodshed seemed to have been in vain, and the position of the people was no better than it had been before—they had exchanged one King for another, but in so doing had merely exchanged the tyranny of birth for that of money. The older writers compromised and accepted the new régime, but there were those—especially amongst the young—who were unable to accept it and they were left in a state of bewilderment in the midst of crashing ideals and tottering loyalties. These young people were what might be called the war generation, that is those who had reached adult life at the time of the July Revolution, having been born and having spent their childhood during the worst years of the Napoleonic era, in an atmosphere of impending doom, in the midst of increasing bad news—lost battles and military disasters. Their parents were weary of war, disgusted with tyranny and despairing of the future, and the children inherited the restlessness and *spleen* of their elders so that, when they reached maturity, they developed a passionate desire to destroy everything and to leave no vestige of the past. The July Revolution had liberated forces of destruction, like an eruption from a volcanic subsoil, like power under pressure, ready to carry away everything in its path to destruction—all customs and habits. Society seemed on the point of disintegration. Fontaney, writing at the time,[1] says: 'I do not anticipate any possible revival for many years to come. If that time ever does come then we ourselves will not be there to see it. Before anything can be rebuilt everything which is still standing must first be razed to the ground, and then the space cleared.'

The section of society first to be attacked was the family, and with it the hierarchy of the sexes. A very striking change arose in the relationship between men and women, and in the attitude of the latter towards the conduct of their own lives. This is not to suggest that women had been mere slaves during earlier centuries. On the contrary, there have been few periods in French history when women have been more important or more influential than during the eighteenth century, or lived—morally speaking—more freely. But they enjoyed this liberty in a man-made world—albeit a world that appreciated women—through the exercise of feminine wiles and feminine diplomacy. Literature has tended to consider the woman of the nineteen-twenties as a modern manifestation which arose as a result of the part she had played during the First World War. But this emancipation had already existed in 1830 and was probably more frequent and more thorough then than in 1920. The bourgeois régime of Louis Philippe and the clericalism of the Second Empire eventually produced a reaction against this modern woman. But before that the Saint-Simonistes had made wide claims for women, and Enfantin, in particular, had never ceased to preach the rehabilitation—or rather the vindication—of woman. 'As long as woman is not seated in the front rank of the hierarchy and has not spoken,' he wrote,[2] 'we must still remain in doubt and uncertainty. . . . The faith which will establish the complete equality of men and women cannot be revealed by man alone.' And again[3]: 'I believe that the definitive moral law can only be revealed by Man *And* Woman and that its application can be the result only of their harmonious action.'

One of the most curious manifestations of the claims for complete spiritual emancipation of woman was the philosophy of a crazy sect called *Évadanistes* who flourished during the early years of the reign of Louis Philippe and they are very typical of the age. Their teaching was sometimes called *Évadisme* and sometimes *Évadaisme*, made from the names of Adam and Eve. It was an androgynous religion composed of male and female elements, and, to compensate woman for the humble part she had hitherto played in the religions of the world, her name, Eve, came first. The leader—or prophet—of this new religion was a man called Ganneau who styled himself *Le Mapah*—a name made from the first syllable of *maman* and the first syllable of *papa*.[4]

Ganneau had two separate and distinct periods in his life. The first, when he was a fashionable spendthrift, which ended when he was about thirty, and the second, a period of almost twenty years—though the first years alone are important—when he was a prophet and even a God.

During the first period he was an elegant young man well known in smart society, and enjoyed gambling, cards, wine and women. On frequent occasions he made large sums of money by gaming and betting, for he seemed to have great luck, but money flowed through his fingers like water. Dumas tells us that, to supplement his income, he used to practise the art, or science, of phrenology. His father had been a hatter and Ganneau, by dint of studying the various sizes and shapes of blocks and hats in his father's workshop, had evolved, with the help of treatises on anatomy, a personal and individual theory of phrenology.

One day, it is said, a very beautiful woman came to consult him to have her fortune read by the bumps on her head. Ganneau was anxious and preoccupied that day; he was sunk in gloom for he had lost a large sum of money at cards, and he did not know what was to become of him. He did not take in the beauty of his consultant, for his thoughts were elsewhere as he was absent-mindedly kneading her skull and talking meanwhile in the slow harmonious voice which was later to mesmerise his followers, but there must have been some unconscious magic in his touch. He was gently stroking the bump at the back of her head which phrenologists call the bump of amorousness, still talking without heeding what he was saying, when, suddenly, she burst into tears and, throwing her arms round his neck, cried: 'I love you!'

Then Ganneau looked at her and, for the first time, saw that she was very beautiful.

After that day she came on several occasions to consult him and he fell in love with her. She was a married woman but they felt that they could no longer live apart and they decided to elope together.

On the day fixed for their flight she came to him covered with jewels and her bag full of pieces of gold, but they were the jewels and the money that her husband had given her, and Ganneau refused to leave with her until she had restituted everything. She came the following day empty-handed, with no money, jewels or clothes, with nothing except what she wore, and they departed together.

They lived happily together and, under her influence, Ganneau gave up gambling. She however later fell ill and died, and he was so stricken with grief that he fell ill also and was thought to be on the point of death. But his beloved one came to him one night as he slept, begged him to live for her sake and to go forth to preach a new religion which should regenerate mankind and whose principles she laid down for him. This was *Évadaisme*.

When Ganneau returned to life he was no longer a man; he had become a God. He was no longer Ganneau, but called himself 'he who was Ganneau'. He was now *Le Mapah*.

As *Le Mapah* he lived in a sordid studio on the Quai de Bourbon in the Ile Saint Louis in Paris, which he called *The Hovel*, and this was his Apostolic Seat. His disciples were artists of all sorts—painters, sculptors and also writers. One adherent who comes as a surprise—whether he was a follower through curiosity or conviction is not known—and that was the Romantic publisher Hetzel, well known for his business sense and for his contracts so merciless to the authors whom he published.

Le Mapah had given up his smart clothes; now he wore a workman's blue linen smock, and with that a battered old felt hat and a woman's long pelisse, which made him look like a dervish. He had a long auburn beard which came down to his navel and his face possessed the majesty of the prophets of old. Most noticeable were his curious hypnotic eyes and his long white, very carefully tended hands which he used gracefully and with great effect.

A portrait of 1834 by Tréviés shows him reclining on a divan and smoking a *chibouk* as he gazes into the distance with mesmeric eyes. He is surrounded by various young men as ecstatic as he.

Eliphas Lévi describes the eloquence of the Master and the magnetic force of his gaze. He says that he expounded his doctrine in biblical and lyrical language which had a certain literary quality—though it was very extravagant in conception and imagery—and it was largely a manifestation of the exaltation of sex and sensuality. He could speak at great length without pausing for rest, but when he had finished there was always a thin rim of white foam at the edge of his lips.

There was always one woman present who looked like a somnambulist, or as if she were in a trance. The *Mapah* used to claim that he was Louis XVI who had come back to earth for 'une œuvre de regénération' and that the woman at his side was Marie-Antoinette.

At first he used to propagate his theories by means of small cabalistic figures made of plaster, but these soon proved too expensive for the slender purse of the prophet, and he replaced them by printed pamphlets which, curiously enough, still continued to bear the name of 'platras'. These pamphlets were decorated with monstrous figures like oriental idols—human figures with elephants' tusks, figures with multiple arms, legs and heads—and they usually ended:

'Au nom du grand Evadah, Au nom du grand Dieu, Mère, Père

A Paris, à l'Univers.

EXPANSION, AMOUR

LE MAPAH.'

The most famous of these 'platras', entitled *Baptême et Mariage*, is to be found in the Bibliothèque Nationale in Paris.[5] It is a long composition in biblical style which sets out to reverse the Christian dogma of the worship of Mary, Mother of God and of Jesus Son of God.

'Mary is no longer the Mother. She is the wife.
Jesus Christ is no longer the son. He is the husband.
The old world (confession) is coming to an end.
The new world (expansion) is about to begin.'

He then goes on to relate how the sacrifice is consummated and declares that a new baptism is at hand, that by the tears of Mary all sin and stain will be washed away and humanity saved. He makes play on the word 'Mary' meaning 'marriage' and the French word for gospel, 'Évangile', meaning 'Ève en germe', the great Mother of Humanity. Mary was once the great God-Mother, now she is the wife of the Man-God of the earth. And with Mary the Mother the *Mapah* places Mary the Whore, Mary-Magdalen. These two are linked together to make one person.

Jesus Christ is greeted in the name of the great *Évadah*, and proclaimed to the world as the great personification of the male unity of the Word and baptised in the name of *Christ-Adam-le-Génésique*. Finally the *Mapah* greets them both together as the great symbol, the personification of unity in duality, under one name *Androgyne-Évadam*.

'Humanity is now constituted for the great bethrothal.
The hour of human virility has come.
The era of *Évadah* is at hand.
    Hosannah!

Given from our Hovel, in our town of Paris, the great *Eda* of
    the earth.
On the first day of the first year of the *Évadah* era,
In the thirty-third year of our age.
    The Mapah.'

The *Mapah* used to send these 'platras' to cabinet ministers to show them where the true life lay. And he once addressed one to Pope Gregory XVI from 'Notre grabat apostolique', telling him that the era of Christianity was at an end, that the *Évadah* era was about to begin, and bidding him stand aside for the great *Mapah*.

Another day he went to a brothel and summoned all the inmates. The girls wondered who he was, this strange man, *Le Mapah*, with the long noble beard, probably some eastern potentate, they thought, who wanted twelve or fifteen women at the same time. 'Ladies' he said to them, 'Do you know who you are?' They giggled and tittered and did not know what to reply, but he did not need an answer. 'You are pioneers,' he said, 'apostles and

martyrs of a new religion.' Then he explained to them in colour-
ful, biblical and esoteric language, that they were the first comers
who were protesting against the vested interest of the honest
woman.

Complaints were frequently sent to the government protesting
against the indecency and obscenity of the *Mapah's* pronounce-
ments, and the prosecutor once considered bringing him to law.
But, when the police came to his hovel to arrest him, he gathered
the folds of his smock round him, like a Roman orator his toga,
and said with great dignity, 'Arrest me! Condemn me! Imprison
me! I'll appeal to the courts! I'll appeal to Humanity!'

The case was not proceeded with. Perhaps the government preferred not to give publicity to his teaching and not to make a
martyr of him.[6]

To most people such manifestos seemed blasphemy of a particularly nasty and salacious kind. It is true that amongst those who
were not spiritually minded these theories led to a glorification of
the flesh and were an encouragement of licence. They tended to
lay stress on aspects of life which Christianity had condemned and
this led to the extolling of sensual indulgence and the worship of
passion. This influenced the conception of love and of the hero
and heroine. The chaste romantic love for Lamartinian Elvires
was now out of date, and the fashionable form was violently
passionate, no longer worship from afar. The object of this burn-
ing love was the 'lionne' who had discarded the flowing draperies
of Elvire which would impede her movements. As the equal—
and even the superior—of man, she despised the frail woman of
the past with her touching ways and slave mentality, her feminine
graces; the *lionne* favoured noisy eccentricity. Like George Sand
she wore corduroy trousers, smoked cigars, or even a pipe, and
was a heavy drinker. Madame d'Agoult, the mistress of Liszt and
mother of Cosima Wagner, who wrote under the pen-name of
Daniel Stern, describes her in her memoirs as 'cavalière, chasse-
resse, bottes éperonnées, fusil à l'épaule, cigare à la bouche, verre
en main, toute impatience et vacarme.'

The young men who were the mates of these new women were
cynical and disillusioned and found everything blighted for them

before they had even lived. Boys of eighteen would repeat a phrase culled from a cheap novel—a phrase which would have delighted the young Baudelaire—'J'ai le cœur usé comme l'escalier d'une fille de joie.'

They were blasphemous and satanic and the words most frequently on their lips were 'Damnation' and 'Hell'. One evening at a café Boccage, the young Romantic actor, in order to shock the company, proposed to his friends that they should play the divinity of Christ in twenty points.[7] While Anatole France tells us that Barbey d'Aurevilly used to say that it was a good thing that Christ was a God since, as a man, he would be pretty feeble.[8]

They professed to despise all decency and to be interested solely in vice and debauch. It was then that every kind of intoxication was practised, that the Artificial Paradises were sought by young men, in an attempt to escape from the lack of hope of their lives. No self-respecting novel of the age but had its orgies, and Balzac describes them as typical of the manners of the day.[9] They revelled in horror, in death and decay, and their favourite reading was the works of the Marquis de Sade and *The Monk* by Lewis, on which they modelled their own works. As Gautier was later to say, in the preface to *Mademoiselle de Maupin*, the 'roman charogne' was fashionable, the literature of the morgue, the prison-cell. It was, he says, a butcher's hallucination, a hangman's nightmare. The taste was for corpses, and the charnel-house was more popular than the boudoir. The fashion was not common to men of letters alone. Berlioz himself tells us of a macabre adventure he had experienced in Florence.[10] One evening in the cathedral he sees a procession of white-robed monks and choristers coming from the sacristy. He asks what they are doing at that late hour at night and is told that they are coming to fetch the body of a young woman who had died in childbirth that afternoon, to take her to the mortuary where she is to spend the night. Berlioz follows them to the house and later back to the cathedral and describes the procession bearing candles through the dark streets, the waving lights, the funeral hymns. They all depart and he is left alone with the undertakers. They open the coffin and, having taken from a smaller one the body of the still-born infant, place it in the arms of the mother.

For a coin pressed into the hand of one of them, Berlioz is allowed to draw near. She is only twenty-two and beautiful, this young woman lying there in her white draperies, her blue eyes half closed and the waves of dark hair round her shoulders. He throws himself on his knees beside her, seizes her hand and covers it with kisses. Then, fearing that the husband might come and imagine that he had been his wife's lover, he leaves the chapel 'tout bouleversé', but cries before he departs, 'Farewell! Farewell! beautiful abandoned wife and shade, but perhaps now consoled, forgive a stranger the tears that he let fall on your pale hand!'

Nature herself staged a macabre drama for the benefit of these young necrophilists in the spring of 1832, in the shape of the cholera which raged from March until November, carrying off, in Paris alone, twenty thousand victims. The horror of the plague did not fade for many years from the minds of Parisians and it seized on the imagination of the public already prone to feast on horror and increased its appetite. It also ensured for some years to come an interest in morbid literature.

For weeks Paris had been waiting with the menace of the plague, which was raging in England, hanging over it and the frivolous members of society, finding the suspense unendurable, took advantage of the carnival to drown their anxiety in uproarious pleasure, and they danced with desperate feverishness as if they thought that they might defy death itself with the extravagance of their dissipation. The tenseness of the atmosphere gave a feverish and unnatural excitement to the festivities, and never had the carnival been more brilliant or more wild. The weather, too, that year was gay and care-free, and spring came earlier than usual with almond blossom of unusual beauty and lilac buds as early as March.

Then, suddenly, in the middle of the Carnival, just as if it had flown into the city hidden under the wings of spring, the plague swept across the Channel and lit on care-free Paris. A harlequin felt an icy hand suddenly clutch at his legs, creep up his body, paralysing his limbs. He tore off his mask in agony and the onlookers saw that his face had already turned purple. Next the whole company of pierrots were struck down by the cholera as they danced. They were carried from the ballroom to the *Hôtel Dieu*, thence immediately to the morgue, and they were buried in their fancy dress, with the powder and paint not washed from their faces. These were the first victims and there were many more soon to follow.

Fontaney, in his *Journal Intime*, gives us a vivid day-to-day account of the progress and ravages of the plague, and it reflects clearly a sensitive man's reactions to the tragedy, a man who was unable, as were so many, to stupefy himself with pleasure and dissipation.

During the months of the plague the hearses used to stand in the streets, like hackney-cabs waiting for hire, and the drivers would go at frequent intervals during the day to ring at the doors of houses, to find out whether there were any dead to bury. They had so many engagements that they were obliged to keep to a strict time-table. Even so there were not sufficient hearses in Paris for the need. Sometimes one saw two or three coffins in the same hearse; sometimes farm carts were seen, and they passed with the coffins piled up like logs of wood; sometimes again furniture-vans were used, and they were crammed to the roof with dead.

Fontaney describes the grim monotony of these processions of hearses and carts, even at night, around the moonlit streets; it seemed like a witches' sabbath, in the beautiful spring nights, for spring continued fine; the chestnuts were in full flower, the laburnum dropped its clusters of golden rain; the lilac gave forth its perfume. The sky remained radiantly blue and the sun continued to shine, with all the buds bursting into flower and the birds singing in the trees. What did Nature care for a few thousand dead?

A favourite pastime was to go to the various cemeteries to see the burials. Enormous trenches were dug that went through old graves and even across streets. Old coffins were dug up to make room for the new, and bones were cast aside, bones with flesh still hanging on them, and even whole bodies in which decomposition had barely set in. These were thrown aside and afterwards flung down on top of the new coffins. The pits were very close together and undertakers were there, with their footrules, measuring the space with great precision, to see that not an inch was wasted. Fontaney describes how, when he was watching a burial, a cough was heard coming from one of the coffins and, when the onlookers insisted on its being opened, it was discovered that the patient was alive, and he was taken back to hospital.

Another pastime, which shows the prevailing love of the macabre, was to go to the *Hôtel Dieu* to watch the pa ients dying of the plague. 'I went to fetch Mérimée' writes Fontaney, 'and we went along to the hospital. We visited all the wards. The patients all looked astonished and terrified, their eyes deeply sunk in their sockets and ringed with black. I saw one old woman who had turned completely purple, with her lips drawn back and showing her teeth. As we went in we saw them carrying down a corpse covered with a sheet. They lay them out in the cellars, on the ground in white sheets. You would imagine they were monks.'

From the *Hôtel Dieu* they went on to a party at Victor Hugo's house in the Place Royale. Liszt was there and he played the Funeral March from Beethoven's piano sonata. 'It was magnificent' says Fontaney, and he imagined the great work which might be created if only the right man would do it, showing all the cholera victims marching, to the sound of the music, draped in their shrouds, through Notre-Dame, at night.

He returned home through the silent moonlit streets, and it was as if Paris were deserted, for scarcely anyone would venture forth after dusk—the people imagined that the plague was more virulent at night. The pest-stricken city lay desolate in the darkness, but every now and then a red lantern would be seen, not the red light of a brothel, but that of a temporary first-aid post. From time to time dark shadows passed in the streets with lanterns, sinister figures carrying coffins. 'Oh! que ces nuits en ces temps de peste sont effrayantes et solennelles' wrote Fontaney.

This atmosphere, the cholera and the spiritual depression, led to despair—either genuine or simulated—as a fashion. The *Spleen* characteristic of Baudelaire is just as typical of the eighteen-thirties. Berlioz, in his memoirs, has a chapter called 'Variétés de Spleen' and he distinguishes between two kinds—the one violent, ironic and bitter, and the other silent, dark and slothful. When the patient is possessed by the latter the end of the world would leave him indifferent. This new characteristic of *spleen* is vastly different from the melancholic 'mal du siècle' of the previous generation. Never was death a more favourite topic for writers than during this period and it is said that the number of suicides increased enormously.[11] *Le Pain des Forts*, written by Alphonse Rabbe, is an apology of suicide. 'One drinks death with pleasure in the wine with which one imagines one is slaking one's thirst; it is eaten with relish in the meals with which one thinks one is nourishing oneself. It has a delicate aroma when one inhales it in a flower or in a perfume.'[12]

Maxime Ducamp was a child during this period and he wrote later in his *Souvenirs*:[13] 'Never was death more loved than then. It was not merely a fashion as one might imagine, it was a general weakness of the spirit which made the heart heavy and sad, which darkened thought and made death welcome as a deliverance. The generation which preceded mine had a youth of despairing sadness, a sadness inherent in their being, in the whole epoch.'

Chapter 2

CARNIVAL

————————————◦◦◦◦◦◦◦◦————————————

The general bankruptcy of spirit did not express itself in *spleen* and despair alone. With the less serious it took the form of eccentricity and frivolity. There have been few periods of history—except a century later, after the First Great War—when life was so hectic, when it took on so desperate a colouring, as during the eighteen-thirties. Then frivolity was a cloak to hide a breaking heart, then it was an opiate to make existence bearable. It was very different from the light-hearted frivolity which was to characterise the Second Empire, the spontaneous bubbling-up of enjoyment in a people who did not realise that their dance-floor bridged the crater of a volcano. Privat d'Anglemont says that people thought of nothing but enjoyment and pleasure. Their fathers had fought too long, had worked too hard, for the sons to care about earning their living, and they thought only of stifling the voice of reason.[1] In the year of the cholera the fever for enjoyment reached new heights. Never was the Carnival more hectic than in 1832 as the population waited anxiously to see whether the plague would fly across the Channel to Paris. It was a regular bacchanalia and the whole of Paris was in the streets—rich and poor. Sweets were flung from carriage to carriage, and rained down on the crowds below; flowers were thrown, and also the first confetti. New devices that year were eggs emptied of their contents through a little hole, and then refilled with flour so that they did not look as if they had been tampered with, but they burst over the heads of the crowd when they were thrown, and covered them as if with snow. The populace used to try to attack and board the carriages of the rich, but these had enlisted the services of hefty porters from the central market, called 'forts de la halle', dressed as Spanish grandees, to throw them off. There were also paid 'engueuleurs', men hired to shout abuse at the other carriages and at the crowd. There were even published pamphlets, which sold in thousands, to teach how to abuse in polite language, without losing one's temper. They were called 'Catéchismes Poissards' and sold like hot cakes.

The highest moment of the Carnival was always, at dawn on Ash Wednesday, the 'Descente de la Courtille', when vagabonds, beggars and tramps poured down from the hills round Paris, and swept into the city through the Porte de Belleville. Fashionable people used to go to watch, and some even took part in the Saturnalia. They used afterwards to declare that it was 'infâme et ignoble', but this did not prevent ladies of the highest rank from returning the following year, and mingling with the prostitutes, pimps and beggars in the streets. They would leave their balls at four o'clock in the morning of Ash Wednesday, still wearing their fancy dress and masks, to get there in time. It is said that eighteen thousand carriages were usually seen there, and sixty thousand people. Anyone who possessed a window near used to let it at a high rent, as if for a royal procession, and many families lived for a whole year on the proceeds alone of these few morning hours. All the low drinking booths near the Courtille were crowded the whole night through and the roofs were even occupied by the time the descent began. The whole peaceful suburb seemed to have changed, overnight, into a witches' Sabbath.

At six o'clock in the morning the annual Descent of the Courtille began. It was like a nightmare vision from Callot, Goya or Hogarth. From the hills the legions of scoundrels and drunkards used to sweep down, gathering further numbers as they drew near Paris. The populace had been drinking all night in their fancy dress and one saw bedraggled and drunken eighteenth-century marquises, pierrots and shepherdesses whirled into the stream, singing obscene songs and shouting wildly. They all swept on and the pale light of dawn began to show up the filthy rags of the beggars and tramps. They used to dance wild dances in which the members of the Jockey Club, the most exclusive club in Paris, used to take part. The ladies of fashion were in their carriages, and the crowds used to hurl insults at them, trying to climb in beside them, while the police were powerless, that morning, to protect them. It was a popular show for which the people had saved up for a whole year, and they would not hear of any of their pleasures being curtailed.

Dancing was the passion of that age, as it is of all ages of turmoil and stress. The wilder and more extravagant the dance the better the public was pleased. The thirties of the nineteenth-century saw the birth of the 'valse éperdue' and the 'galop infernal'. A German visitor to Paris, at the time, describes this galop.[2] 'The rhythm of the music gains in speed and the gestures of the dancers become more passionate, more urgent and more insistent. The whole dance changes in character and becomes 'une course effrénée' in which the couples stampede down the whole length of the hall. The attitude and expression of the dancers show 'un embrasement si voluptueux' as the rout grows wilder and wilder, that it gives the impression of a witches' Sabbath. The rhythm of the music becomes still more rapid while the women, their faces red from the exertion, their mouths half open, their hair in wild disarray, are dragged panting along, rather than upheld by their legs, until finally they fall with the crashing of the last chord on the nearest chair'.

The most characteristic dance of the period was the *Cancan*, very different then from the innocent dance it was later to become, and which was considered highly indecent by the more respectable members of society. It was first danced in Paris in 1831 at a low tavern haunted by soldiers and sailors, and was said to have been brought to France from Algeria by troops returning on leave. Its chief characteristics seem to have been the obscenity and lasciviousness of the gestures and movements of the dancers. This was increased if the participants were intoxicated, as they often were in the low places where it was usually danced. It was first introduced into smart society at the notorious and hysterical Carnival of 1832. With Roger de Beauvoir and Count d'Alton

Shée, Charles La Battut danced it at the ball at the theatre of Les Variétés.[3]

The great event of the Carnival was always the ball at Les Variétés. People used to spend fortunes on their costumes and often ruined themselves in the process. It was as if, in the guise of a historical character, they were able to forget the problems which were besetting them. At the masked fancy dress ball at Les Variétés any licence was countenanced.

That year, in 1832, in the midst of the dancing, a flood of intoxicated young men, arm in arm, were seen to hurl themselves down the temporary stairs which led from the Grand Circle to the Orchestra Stalls which was occupied by the dance floor. They swept through the crowd of dancers, dragging along in their torrent everything which stood in their way. Suddenly the chain broke up and the disguised and masked young men scattered through the hall, seizing girls away from their partners by main force and dancing wildly with them, making bawdy jokes and brazen advances to them. Their previous partners were outraged and some of the respectable members of the company were disgusted at this flaunting of absence of all decorum and decency, though the young women, the victims of this assault, were almost all delirious with excitement and enjoyment. Finally, to the horror of some of the public, La Battut began to dance the *Cancan*. The police made vain efforts to stop the dance but they could do nothing in face of the torrent of popular acclamation, and they had to allow it to sweep along to its victorious conclusion.

The following morning La Battut was visited by the manager of Les Variétés who assured him that the police would not molest him again, and begged him to return that evening to his ball and, by dancing the *Cancan*, to renew the fantastic success of the previous evening. The police authorites had given way before the general approval, and they were relieved, in any case, by this safety-valve for overwrought feelings, and thought it more welcome than other forms of insubordination. Apart from the anxiety over the cholera, there was much political unrest and opposition to the new régime, with disturbances and strikes which were taking on the importance of minor revolutions. It was not at all certain, at this time, that the dynasty would survive and the government was glad of any diversion.

La Battut had, however, other plans for that evening, and he went with Roger de Beauvoir and d'Alton Shée to the ball at the Théâtre de l'Odéon where they smuggled in a naked dancer. She slipped in past the doorkeeper draped in the voluminous folds of a shawl, well flanked and hidden by a group of young men. Once inside, like Salome, she discarded her veils, but this did not take her long as she had only one, and appeared naked, except for a feather boa and long black gloves. Then she began to dance the *Cancan*. The effect was instantaneous. All the young men in the hall crowded round her from all sides, shouting 'Vive Vénus! Vive Vénus!' The police on duty rushed forward, waving their batons excitedly and tried to put an end to this scandalous 'outrage aux mœurs', but they were driven back and had to beat a hasty retreat beneath the blows which rained on them from all sides. Then the dancer, taking advantage of the confusion, draped herself once more in her shawl and disappeared with her escort.

Houssaye, comparing the audacious licence which was the fashion in the early eighteen-thirties with the frivolity of the Second Empire wrote 'the reasonable "folies" of today seem a mere funeral procession compared with the "folies abracadabran-tesques" which Musard used to conduct with his fiddles which seemed possessed by the Devil. They were a storm, a whirlwind, a tornado'.[4]

This Musard, of whom Houssaye here writes, was one of the most characteristic figures of the early years of the reign of Louis Philippe. He symbolised in himself the frenzied quality of the years between 1830 and 1836. It was he who conceived the 'valse éperdue' and the 'galop infernal'. He was the conductor of the dance orchestra at Les Variétés during the Carnival of 1832. It was the febrile atmosphere of that year which started his vogue.

Philippe Musard, or as he is usually called, Napoléon Musard, 'cet empereur du carnaval,'[5] was a little man of somewhat undis-tinguished appearance—or seemed so until he stood before his orchestra. He was generally shabby, with ill-kept hair, dressed almost invariably in an ill-fitting black suit buttoned to the neck, showing only a thin line of white collar. He looked like a page-boy, somewhat like the Fat Boy from *The Pickwick Papers*. Yet this grotesque and burlesque little man managed to enjoy the most phenomenal popularity in his day. During the years of his vogue no Christmas was complete without the windows of confectioners showing countless little Musards made of chocolate, marzipan or ginger-bread.

It was generally believed that he was possessed by the Devil, that he had made a pact with the Prince of Darkness, for this alone could explain how he came to conceive the 'galop infernal'. That galop, Balzac used to say, needed the help of Satan. According to the contemporary legend he could summon evil spirits from Hell.

> 'Ce Musard infernal,
> C'est Satan qui conduit le bal!'

The date of his birth is not known but he was said to be sixty-six at the time of his death in 1859. He is alleged to have begun his musical career by playing the horn at low working-class 'hops'. At that time he was also composing quadrilles which were the fashionable dance then.

During the Restoration he went to England to make his fortune, and it was in London that he reached a certain modicum of fame by organising the court balls and leading the orchestra. In England he was not satisfied with being a mere bandsman, but had the ambition of becoming a writer of classical music and wrote only serious works.

After the Revolution of 1830 he returned to Paris and published some of his serious works—several string quartets and three parts of his treatise on composition, *Nouvelle Méthode de Composition Musicale*. However the path of the serious musician is hard and stony, and progress was slow, but he was to reach fame by another road. The extravagant Carnival of 1832 gave him his chance, and he was largely responsible for the success of the balls at Les Variétés. As the result of this, a man with capital conceived the plan of organising public concerts and dances in the Champs Elysées and he entrusted their direction to Musard. Musard eventually quarrelled with his employer but, by that time, he was so well known that he could afford to launch out on his own. First at the Jardin Turcq, next at the Salle Saint Honoré and finally, when he had amassed sufficient capital, he built his own dance hall which he opened in 1836. It enjoyed immediate success and became soon the vogue of fashionable Paris.

Musard was now one of the most important figures in Paris. He was managing the balls at the Opéra Comique and at the Salle Saint Honoré, as well as those at his own dance hall. So important was he then that the false rumour of his death in 1837 created general consternation and a feeling of universal grief.

'Who has not seen Musard' writes the reporter to the Menestral,[6] 'at the balls at the Opera has not really lived. There, standing on the Venetian bridge in the light of a thousand candles, the Maestro is his true self. He is no longer a man, not even a musician, but a God who is conducting the orchestra. Sometimes he rolls his eyes round like balls of fire; sometimes he gazes from right to left with serenity and calm. His bow, which never grows weary, seems to draw each note—from the majestic semibreve to the tripping quaver—and to lead it right to the very centre of his listener's ear. With one single glance he can hypnotise those around him, with his bow gather back those who have wandered, restrain those ready to escape, warn those whose attention flags, and rouse those who have lagged behind. In the *allegros* and the *andantes*, on the contrary, his glance seems to dart lightning, his nerves are taut and his whole body seems to be the incarnation of that ideal conception, perpetual motion. Then he is no longer beating time. He is hacking it out with repeated blows, with his feet, his hands, his elbows, with his knees, with his whole body.

'Sometimes he stands rigid, gazing at the ceiling, looking down at his public from the full height of his majesty, scratches his head, pats his ribs; sometimes he sits down and wearily passes his hand across his brow. Sometimes the tip of his bow seems to hover over the note just as it is dying away, helping it, as it were, to its death; at other times the bow seems to pick the note up from the floor and to summon it back to the music-desk.'

All these movements were in time with the music which the orchestra was playing. Whatever he was doing, his baton or his bow was not a mere baton or bow, but a magician's wand. He had a very individual manner of leading the orchestra, says Pougin, of communicating to it his satanic quality. With his band composed of twenty-four first and second violins, with a suitable number of violas and 'cellos, twelve trombones and cornets, he was able to achieve many striking effects which have not been without influence on the development of even serious music. He is said to have been the first to have tried the experiment of giving the tune to the brass wind, not being content to use it solely for the inner parts of the orchestration. In another aspect also he left his mark for he may be considered the father, the grandfather, or the great-grandfather of modern jazz. In order to enhance the stimulating power of his music he resorted to effects which were not in themselves musical; he used the sound of breaking wood, of repercussion on non-resonant surfaces, of pistol shots fired off in time with the music. Some of these originated by chance. Once during one of his numbers the chair on which a member of his orchestra was seated suddenly broke and the sound of the cracking wood happened to harmonise with the beat of the music. The public thought that here was an intentional effect, a new Musard stunt, and they were ecstatic in their appreciation. As soon as the dance was over he was carried in triumph round the hall. This dance was subsequently called 'le galop de la chaise cassée', and it remained one of the creator's outstanding achievements. Later he varied the effect by firing off pistol shots at regular intervals, by banging on his desk with his baton in time with the music, and many other similar stunts.

By this time Musard had abandoned original composition and his music consisted largely of a *pot-pourri* of popular tunes of the day, or tags from well-known popular operas, but what was original was his manner of treating the material which he borrowed from others.

His most famous creations were quadrilles rather than galops, and these were pageants more than mere dances. He invented fancy-dress quadrilles with subjects drawn from French history—from the Middle-Ages and the Renaissance. He created quadrilles also from foreign countries—English, Spanish, Arab and so forth

—and many other varieties of quadrilles. He composed the *Paris Students Quadrille*, the *Pirates Quadrille* and the *Quadrille de la Reine des Fous*. There were others like *The Whirlwind*, *The Thunderstorm* and a variety of others.

The most famous perhaps of all these quadrilles was the *Quadrille des Huguenots*, described by Delphine de Girardin.[7] 'The *Quadrille des Huguenots* is a wonderful spectacle; nothing more fantastic can be imagined. The lights in the hall fade away and are replaced by a reddish glow to simulate the flames of the fires. It is a strange sight to see all the happy faces, all this gaiety against the macabre background. Then all these noisy ghosts, these demons of joy and madness, begin to move in long columns, they dash along in torrents, they turn and twist, sweeping backwards and forwards; the couples crowd together, surge forward and back, without ceasing, never stopping, and the tocsin tolls, and the tumtum of the drums rolls. The orchestra plays on; it hammers out the beat, growing louder and more insistent, never allowing the dancers any respite or breathing space; the volleys of the guns ring out at regular intervals, cries and groans are heard. It is truly civil war; it is massacre itself. The illusion is perfect.'

Musard's immense success with the balls at the theatre of the Variétés opened for him the doors of the Opera. This was a great honour and a revolutionary change. Up to that time no fancy-dress balls had been permitted there as they were considered vulgar. The only mark of festivity had been the masks worn by the ladies. What was called the 'débraillé' of the period, 'l'orgie Musard', had been stemmed by the gates of the Opera. In 1836, when Musard entered there, it was as if the Barbarians had broken into a sacred temple. But the Opera had to yield to him, for everyone was dancing at his balls while those at the Opera were deserted. Mira, the director of these balls, had tried every kind of device—dignified devices—to make them more popular and to compete with the excitement elsewhere, but in vain. The taste of the public had been blunted, it had grown accustomed to 'l'orgie Musard' and it could no longer appreciate any less highly spiced fare. Mira then entreated the governing body to grant him permission to give a fancy-dress ball and to employ Musard. This was granted, but on the day preceding that on which the ball was to be held, the authorities, seized with panic, rescinded the permission. Mira would not consider himself beaten, and continued to advertise his ball and to sell the tickets. The whole day of the ball he spent wrangling with the governors and they finally yielded, but only at seven o'clock in the evening, under pressure from the subscribers who threatened to batter down the gates of the Opera if they were deprived of their fancy-dress ball. The authorities gave way and the ball was held, but the Opera is a state theatre and the following day they were fined ten thousand francs. It is said however that the fine was never collected.

It was at this first ball at the Opera that Musard, in one of his quadrilles, fired off a small trench mortar, and this caused a sensation even greater than that of the broken chair. The smell of gunpowder seemed to intoxicate the dancers, so that they shouted, stampeded and finally, seizing Musard, bore him in triumph down the hall.

Delphine de Girardin quotes two letters written to her by friends describing the events of this ball from opposing standpoints.[8] 'I regret very much' wrote the first correspondent 'that your attack of influenza prevented you from going last night to the Musard ball at the Opera. Nothing could give you an adequate conception of what it was like. There were six thousand people present in the hall and two thousand were refused admission at the door. All the boxes were taken and even those of the King and the Duke of Orleans were invaded by the mob who had nowhere else to go. The dresses were most lavish and picturesque; the dances lovely and most passionate. Musard was carried in triumph on the shoulders of six of the handsomest men round the hall, while the whole company loudly acclaimed him, cheering vociferously. Musard's face was glowing with happiness. He is certainly "roi des ribauds".'

The second letter gives the converse point of view. 'You were quite right not to go to the *Bal Musard* last night at the Opera House,' it said. 'There was the most appalling crush imaginable. It is difficult to conceive how people can enjoy such pleasures. There were many battles and we were in considerable danger.

A FANCY DRESS BALL IN THE
EIGHTEEN THIRTIES
After a lithograph by Achille Devéria

In the galop a young man slipped and fell while the whole rout passed over his prostrate body. He was picked up afterwards in a most shocking condition. As far as I personally was concerned the tails of my coat were ripped off my back. I did not write to you immediately to give you the details of this shocking wild ball because I thought it wiser that it should not be widely discussed.'

In the meantime Musard continued on his triumphal course and Delphine de Girardin, writing an account of his balls for a paper the following year, said:[9] 'Paris is dancing! Paris is jigging! Paris is enjoying itself in every possible way. Everyone is tearing as hard as possible for Ash Wednesday will soon be upon us. Every quarter of Paris is in uproar. The *Faubourg Saint Honoré* is jigging! "Il tourne, il roule, il se rue, il se précipite, il s'abîme, il tourbillonne, il fond comme une avalanche!" It sweeps round you like a monsoon. It is hell let loose! It is Bedlam on the spree! It is Mazeppa on his mad horse! It is Leonora carried away by her lover, through the forests, the deserts, over rocks, stopping only to die! It is a nightmare, a witches' Sabbath! The *Galop Musard* is an awesome pleasure! The fancy-dress balls at the *Salle Saint Honoré* are as fashionable this year as last year.'[10]

Chapter 3

THE DANDIES

There were some who tried to escape from the pervading feeling of futility and from the growing materialism of the age; these were the Dandies who endeavoured to make of their own lives a thing of beauty, a work of art set high above the vulgar world around them, They dissociated themselves from the common life of moneymaking and prided themselves on their idleness, on their uselessness, since they considered that everything which was useful could only be ugly. Baudelaire, himself a Dandy, was later to say:[1] 'To be a useful man has always seemed to me something very hideous indeed!' The cult of self, with the Dandies, took the place of religion—they were professed free-thinkers for the greater part—and their narcissism arose from their inability to find in the life around them any idealism or nobility. So they cultivated themselves, developed themselves, for the sole purpose of making of themselves and their lives a work of art. For this end they tended their personal appearance, gave time and thought to the choice of their clothes so that they should be as different as possible from those of the bourgeoisie. This led to eccentricity, though they were never as wildly extravagant as the members of the *Petit Cénacle*, for they did not think it necessary to become 'débraillé' in order to give proof of originality. Arsène Houssaye, who was a Dandy but also lived amongst the members of the *Petit Cénacle* when they became the *Bouzingos*, used to declare that he thought it was quite right that Gautier should wear a frock-coat with brandenburghs, that Gérard de Nerval should dress like Werther, that Ourliac should wear Cossack boots, but, as far as he was concerned, he thought one could be a Romantic writer even if one dressed like everyone else.[2] The literary Dandies did not, however, as Houssaye's words might lead one to believe, dress like everyone else, even if they did not adopt the fancy-dress extravagance of the *Petit Cénacle*—witness the clothes worn by Nestor Roqueplane, Roger de Beauvoir and Barbey d'Aurevilly, of which more will be spoken later. They certainly did not wish to dress as did the bourgeoisie, and their clothes, even when they were fantastic, were always most carefully planned down to the last detail, and were never the result of chance.

The fathers of many of the Dandies had spent some years in England during the Revolution and the Napoleonic Wars, and had developed a 'snobisme' towards English manners and traditions. This gave them distinction and proved that they could not belong to the new bourgeoisie. They still further exaggerated this Anglomania, and the ideal that they set before themselves was the English one of impassivity and reluctance to express emotion. They also adopted the bad manners of the English well-bred, manners very unlike the traditional well-bred French manners, composed as they were of arrogance, lack of consideration for others—or even awareness of them—particularly for those who were not of their own social class, whom they treated with hauteur and insolence.

Fashion required that the Dandy should drive his own car, the ubiquitous tilbury, and that he should be accompanied by a diminutive groom called a 'tiger', who sat up on the back seat with folded arms and tried to emulate the arrogance of expression of his master. He was usually no more than nine or ten years old since he must not exceed three feet in height; he had to have iron nerves and to be as agile as a squirrel to be ready to spring down from his perch at the call of his master. He usually drank and was adept at swearing. It was fashionable at that time for the 'tiger' to be Irish and to be called Paddy or Timmy. It was also an advantage if he were known to be vicious or depraved.

The height of ambition for the Dandy was to be elected a member of the Jockey Club, the most exclusive club in Paris and as exclusive as an English Club. On Carnival days the members would sit at the windows and gaze disdainfully down at the people enjoying themselves in the streets below.

The most famous members of the Club in the thirties were the Marquis de Saint Cricq and the Englishman Lord Henry Seymour, the founder of the Club, round whom all the other members gravitated and on whom they modelled themselves. The height of every member's ambition was to get to know them and to be seen in their company.

In the early eighteen-thirties every kind of eccentricity flourished, and the delight of being absurd in public places, of trying to 'épater le bourgeois' was very typical of the Dandies. At that time extravagant conduct began to be accepted as the hall-mark of independence, intelligence and breeding. Well known are the peculiarities of behaviour of the Marquis de Saint Cricq; so great were these that it might almost seem that he was somewhat mad, if the accounts can be believed. Villemessant says[3] that he used to arrive at the Café Tortoni, order tea and then empty the contents of the salt-cellar into the pot. After tasting the beverage he would pronounce it undrinkable, complain at being given such tea, and demand some fresh. At that time tea cost a hundred francs a pound, that is about four pounds in the currency of the day. Another day he clad himself in a peasant's smock and wooden shoes, then marched at the head of a caravan of empty cabs which he had hired for the purpose, along the boulevard until he reached the Café Anglais; there he halted his caravan and ordered it to wait while he went to drink and play cards with his friends.

Roger de Beauvoir who knew him well said that he was not mad, or even eccentric, but that he had so great a contempt for the general public that he wanted to see how much it would swallow with open-mouthed astonishment, and the more he astounded it the more he despised it.[4] De Beauvoir once heard him from his box at the Comédie Française shouting during a very bad play, 'Thirty-thousand francs for the author!' and again repeatedly, 'I demand thirty-thousand francs for the author!' When at last someone enquired why he wanted so large a reward for so bad a play, he answered: 'He might then stop writing plays!'

Roger de Beauvoir gives another version of the Villemessant story of the empty cabs. He relates that one evening at the theatre Saint Cricq was so much disgusted at the applause which greeted a very bad play that, in the interval, he went out and hired all the cabs waiting outside. It was a very wet night and he had ensured that none of the smartly dressed men and women of the audience would be able to go home under cover. At the close of the play they applauded more vociferously than ever and he shouted at them from his box: 'Clap away, fools that you are, you'll all get soaked going home!'

Lord Henry Seymour, although he passed in Paris for an Englishman, was not wholly English and he had never been to England. He was the illegitimate son of the Marchioness of Hertford by Casimir de Montrond, the friend of Talleyrand. Earlier, de Montrond had married Aimée de Coigny, Duchesse de Fleury, the 'Jeune Captive' of Chénier's poem, whom he saved from the guillotine and who had married him out of gratitude. The marriage did not however turn out a success and she left him after five years. The Marquis of Hertford, when he was Lord Yarmouth, had been in France during the Napoleonic wars and was once arrested by the French authorities as an English spy. While he was in prison his wife lived in Paris in order to be able to visit him, and it was then that she became the mistress of Casimir de Montrond. It is even said that the latter obtained the release of her husband so that she could claim, with some appearance of verisimilitude, that the child to be born in January 1805 was his. Lord Yarmouth however was not taken in by this subterfuge and never believed that the boy was his, although he could not refuse him his name. Lord Henry's large fortune did not come to him from his father who left him nothing but his name, but from his mother who had been in the curious position of having two rich men claiming to be her father—George Selwyn and the Marquis of Queensberry both of whom left her great wealth. The matter had been taken to the Courts and the case had been decided in favour of Selwyn but Queensberry did not feel bound by this decision, and he could not, in any case, be prevented from making a will in favour of the woman he believed to be his daughter.

Lady Hertford, in her old age, lived in a house in Paris of which she let off the ground floor to the Café de Paris, but she enjoyed her tenants so much that she never asked them for any rent. Her sole companion in later years was a youth called Richard Wallace who passed for her nephew, but who was generally believed to be her illegitimate son. On the death in 1870 of his reputed cousin, Richard Seymour, the half-brother of Henry Seymour, he inherited a large fortune and also a number of magnificent works of art which have become the Wallace Collection. Wallace had tried to leave them to France, for he was an ardent Francophile who served on the French side during the Franco-Prussian War, but had been prevented by some clause in the will. During the siege of Paris he gave two hundred thousand francs for coal and wood for the poor of Paris, and forty thousand meal tickets. Later he gave to the French government the sum to build the drinking fountains which are still seen in some of the squares of Paris. The Provisional Government of 1871 was less generous to him and his only reward was to have two species of camellia in the Jardin des Plantes called after him. This is however much later history.

In the eighteen-thirties Lord Henry Seymour was a gloomy young man who was always impeccably dressed and exquisitely arrogant. The Anglomania of the period, his title and his wealth, and also his superb arrogance gave him notoriety. In 1833 he founded a society to encourage the breeding of pedigree horses in France; this became the Jockey Club in 1835 under his presidency, but he resigned two years later because he did not approve of the pastimes of the other members. He had never intended that his Club should become the resort of men who spent their days in idleness, gambling and drinking. He himself was interested only in physical exercise and he had the deepest contempt for art and letters. He spent his immense fortune largely on sport, and he was an expert in all forms of physical activity—boxing and wrestling, riding and shooting, racing and fencing. He had his own private gymnasium where he spent many hours each day with instructors of physical culture, and he was very proud of his muscular development. Villemessant describes the thickness of his arm which had the span of a woman's waist.

76

There was something bitter and sadistic in his temperament, and he delighted in humiliating even his closest friends. He made fashionable in Paris the cruel practical joke which is a characteristic feature of the period, and was considered the distinguishing mark of the nobleman. His idea of fun was to put purgatives in the wine which he served to his friends, and to sprinkle their clothes with itching powder.

He passed into the French tradition as the typical English aristocrat, and his cruel practical jokes, his sardonic wit, his physical prowess, and his lavish expenditure were the model of the Dandies. Not that all the exploits attributed to him were really his—he would not perhaps have been so showy—they were in fact mostly those of Charles la Battut who had as much right to be called English as had Lord Henry Seymour.

Charles la Battut was the illegitimate son of an English chemist of great wealth and he was born in 1806. The chemist, unable to marry his mistress, paid a large sum of money to an impoverished Breton nobleman to recognise the child as his and to give him his name. On the death of the chemist Charles la Battut inherited a large fortune which he proceeded to squander rapidly in Paris. His ambition was to earn a notorious reputation at the time when the Marquis de Saint Cricq and Lord Henry Seymour were making notoriety fashionable. Many are the fantastic tales which are told of his exploits. The Paris mob perhaps suspected that he was trying to buy fame with money—it is quick to sense falseness and pretentiousness—for it would never allow him any notoriety of his own. However wild were his extravagances he was never given credit for them, for the crowd all shrieked: 'Vive Lord Seymour! Vive Milord Arsouille!'* It is not known whether the epithet refers to Lord Henry himself or only to his imitator.

The turbulent and tempestuous carnivals between 1832 and 1835 were the period of la Battut's exploits. On the last Sunday before Lent his large landau would appear on the boulevards in the midst of crowds of merry-makers in their fancy dress. It was preceded by two outriders looking like picadors, and sounding a loud fanfare on immense hunting horns wound round their bodies.

* Arsouille = Debauchee.

The coachman and footmen were decked in multi-coloured favours, and the carriage was thronged with young men and women, standing up and flinging confetti on to the mob below, and handfuls of coins which were immediately scrambled for. When evening fell the carriage was lit up by torches, and everywhere it passed the crowds yelled 'Vive Lord Seymour! Vive Milord Arsouille!' Working people and respectable bourgeois stood still in the streets and marvelled at the extravagance of the English lord. In point of fact Lord Henry always denied that he had ever been to the carnival.

By 1835 Charles la Battut had spent the whole of his large fortune. He is said to have left France and to have gone to Naples where he died shortly afterwards unknown and penniless. He was then only twenty-nine.[5]

Some of the exploits of the Dandies were genuinely amusing. Paris chuckled for many weeks over the trick played on the authorities by the journalist Nestor Roqueplane on the night of the ball given by the King for the marriage of the heir apparent, the Duke of Orleans.[6] Louis Philippe, as befitted a monarch who prided himself on his democratic principles, gave a ball at the Hôtel de Ville, and he invited members of all classes of society. When Roqueplane arrived in the vicinity of the Hôtel de Ville so great was the throng of carriages that he soon realised that he would not reach the ballroom until the early hours of the morning, for they were proceeding at a snail's pace. He did not intend to remain five or six hours sitting in his cab. He returned home, sent for a stretcher and two stretcher bearers. He lay down on it, dressed for the ball, covered himself with a blanket so that nothing could be seen except the tip of his nose. Then he ordered the bearers to carry him to the Hôtel Dieu, the hospital standing in the square opposite the Hôtel de Ville. As soon as he again reached the vicinity of the town hall he got involved with the slow-moving traffic, and the stretcher-bearers were told that they could proceed no further. But, at their cry, 'a dying man for the Hôtel Dieu' a way was made for them through the crowd of carriages, and in this manner Roqueplane arrived in the square. He then skipped off his stretcher, throwing aside the blanket, and, to the amazement of the onlookers, ran up the steps of the Hôtel de Ville and arrived in perfectly good time.

Nestor Roqueplane was an ugly little man who nevertheless managed to charm everyone and he was almost the most popular person in Paris from 1830 until his death in 1870. In spite of the homeliness of his appearance he was a Dandy and it was he who introduced the fashion for coloured stripes running down the side seams of the trousers.[7] He used to say that when he had a fitting for a new suit next day he could not sleep the previous night on account of his nervousness and anxiety.

Like Baudelaire he was happy only in Paris and he was a well-known figure in the cafés, where he sat and told stories and anecdotes by the score. He used to say that even the trees hated the country for they too migrated to Paris—and he then pointed to the carts laden with tree trunks passing.

The glitter of these big names of the eighteen-thirties has in the course of time grown tarnished. Who remembers now the Marquis de Saint Cricq, Lord Henry Seymour, Charles la Battut or Nestor Roqueplane? The only names which still have sparkle are those of men who were not merely Dandies and eccentrics, but were also known in literature—Roger de Beauvoir and particularly Barbey d'Aurevilly.

Roger de Beauvoir's name is met everywhere in the memoirs and letters of the eighteen-thirties. He was born with the plain surname of Roger but added de Beauvoir to it from the name of his country property. He was endowed by nature with many gifts. He was good-looking and elegant, witty and clever, and moreover had a private income of fifteen hundred pounds a year. He was a member of the Jockey Club and kept a fashionable tilbury and groom. He was the idol of the young men of the day who tried to emulate him. Everywhere he went people made room for him and when he appeared, sparkling with vitality, dressed in his famous tight-fitting sky-blue coat with the golden buttons, the primrose-coloured waistcoat and the pearl-grey trousers; with his pointed beard and his dark curling hair, he was said by his contemporaries to resemble a nobleman who had stepped down from a picture by Paolo Veronese. His *Écolier de Cluny* obtained great popularity when it appeared in 1832. It was in the best charnel-house tradition, but unfortunately the subject was subsequently stolen from him by Dumas for his *Tour de Nesle*. De Beauvoir wrote as well a considerable number of works which enjoyed a certain amount of success in his day, but which are now forgotten. He was gifted and with his talents he might have become a good—even a great—writer if he had allowed himself the time to work, and if he had not wasted so many precious hours and so much money on wine and women. Every night of his life he was to be seen in the green-room of some theatre, paying court to some leading lady. There was no important function to which he was not invited, for his good-humour and his wit made him a popular guest. His latest joke or 'bon mot' was always on everybody's lips, and these were the more notorious by the slight element of spite which they contained.

His house was one of the most famous of the day and was even described in the weekly *La Mode*[8]—the height of fame. In true Romantic manner he had a Gothic room hung with black velvet hangings spangled with silver, and the furniture was of old carved oak; in one corner stood an antique Prie-Dieu, though Roger de Beauvoir was never known to pray, and on its ledge was a missal said to date from the sixteenth century. His drawing-room was hung with light coloured velvet, the furniture consisted of museum pieces of the period of Louis XV; there were scrolled and gilded mirrors on the walls and glass-doored cabinets filled with priceless china. The parqueted floors were covered with old eastern rugs.

In the early forties Roger de Beauvoir migrated across the river to the Ile Saint-Louis which was then more isolated than now, for no real bridges united it with the mainland, only foot-bridges. It was self-contained like a small provincial town. He rented a flat in the beautiful Hôtel Lauzun which had been built in the sixteen-fifties for Charles de Gruyn, and in 1682 passed into the hands of the Duc de Lauzun whose name it now bears, and whose adventures with La Grande Mademoiselle, the daughter of Gaston of Orleans, are well known. Roger de Beauvoir describes the house as an old Venetian palace on the banks of the Seine. It is in the

Hôtel Lauzun that the Club des Haschichins used to meet at this time, and which is described by Gautier.[9] Any bourgeois, if he could have entered the precincts of this club, would have been terrified and horrified at the sight of the members sitting solemnly round the table waving Renaissance daggers and swords above their heads, and bending over a bowl of astonishing-looking green jam, whose colour the flickering light of the candles made more ghostly.

De Beauvoir's rooms were on the second floor, on the front, with a balcony which enjoyed a lovely view. To the right it looked towards the Arsenal and to the left it commanded the whole extent of the river as far as the Tuileries. In the sitting-room there were panels and a ceiling painted by Le Sueur and in the bedroom another ceiling, by the same artist, represented 'Sleep'. In this house he gave a house-warming to six hundred guests which was long remembered. He records it himself.[10]

> *Et la Seine déjà reflète en germes folles*
> *Le lustre de l'hôtel aux vieilles girandoles.*
> *Puis la fête s'éteint aux premiers feux du jour.*

From Roger de Beauvoir's windows there was a view of the open-air baths near the Hôtel Lauzun, and, from time to time, a pretty girl could be seen going or coming from there. One day, as he sat on his balcony with Musset, Arago and the banker Mosselmann, he saw a young woman coming from the baths, with wonderful copper-coloured hair hanging down her shoulders, damp from her swim and glinting in the sunlight. Then, struck by her beauty, he ran downstairs to invite her to his rooms.[11] This was Apollonie Aglaé Sabatier whom Baudelaire was to love and for whom he was to write his most spiritual poems. But this was many years after her first visit to the Hôtel Lauzun.[12]

Barbey d'Aurevilly is today the best remembered of the Dandies, largely because it was he who crystallised the personality of the Dandy in his monograph *Du Dandyisme et de Georges Brummel*, but in the eighteen-thirties he was less fashionable and famous than Roger de Beauvoir. He himself recognised this supremacy with which he could not compete through lack of means, and

F   *81*   S.P.B.

saw in him the most worthy follower of his English ideal—both in his manner of living and dressing.

Barbey d'Aurevilly, as a young man, had once seen Beau Brummel at the end of his life when he was British Consul at Caen, and ever since he had been obsessed by the memory of his personality and by the ambition of emulating him. This seemed to him far more important than fame in literature. He was eventually to make a name as a novelist—curiously enough as a realist—but his best work, *Une Vieille Maîtresse*, was not published until 1854. When *Du Dandyisme et de Georges Brummel* appeared in a limited edition in 1844, he had only published two trifles—*L'Amour Impossible* and *La Bague d'Annibal*. He had a small private income which he supplemented through free-lance journalism, and he expended his energies largely on the creation of his personality on the model of Georges Brummel, an artificial personality. 'If one were passionate' he said 'one would be too real to be a Dandy.'[13] This personality was created largely through his clothes; he spent all his money on them and was never able to afford, as Roger de Beauvoir could, a setting suitable for his creation and so he lived all his life in cheap hotels or mean lodgings. In the eighteen-thirties he chose his manner of dressing and kept it until the day of his death when he was over eighty. At first it was only a slight exaggeration of the then prevailing fashion, but fifty years later he seemed always to be wearing fancy dress. He continued to wear these clothes devised by him and whose cut he had supervised, as a protest against ready-mades, the reach-me-downs of a machine-made age.

The most important event of his day was his toilet and his dressing; he used to spend several hours in his bath, and every day the hair-dresser came to wave his hair and to set it in curls round his forehead. In his diary he writes: 'Did many things today, amongst others my toilet. Tried on a pair of trousers and ordered a coat. Grave matters, almost religious!'[14]

On account of the care he took with his appearance Lamartine used to call him the Duc de Guise of literature.

His costume was composed of a tight-fitting frock-coat, padded at chest and shoulders, with fluted skirts and pinched-in waist. To

achieve the desired narrowness he wore what was virtually a
corset—a whale-boned waistcoat—and this constriction prevented
him from eating much when he was dressed. 'I ate nothing out of
respect for the whale-bones of my waistcoat' he said. And another
time 'If I were to receive Communion I'd burst.'[15] With the frock-
coat he wore a waistcoat of bright green or pale blue velvet, a lace
jabot and wide lace cuffs fastened by jewelled links. He wore
tight-fitting white trousers and he followed Nestor Roqueplane's
fashion of having a stripe of blue, pink or yellow running down
the side seams. With all this he wore a wide cloak and a large-
brimmed black hat lined underneath with red velvet. In his belt
was stuck a dagger. He also wore black gloves with gold stitching.

He was well-known in his day for the affectation and preciosity
of his speech. 'I immolate a rose every evening' he said once, 'a
rose is the *Order of Merit* of that great sovereign whom we call
Nature.'[16] He was also famous for his 'bons mots', for his wit and
irony. 'Irony' he said,[17] 'is a form of genius which dispenses with
the need of any other—with the need of heart or commonsense.'

The weakness of the ideal of Dandyism as formulated by Barbey
d'Aurevilly was that it led often to pomposity, to lack of humour,
and to the Dandy taking himself too seriously. Barbey d'Aurevilly
himself realised this eventually, for he then wrote, 'The Dandy
lives on his dignity as on a pole; this naturally somewhat impedes
his liberty of movement and makes him stiff in his demeanour.'[18]

Theoretically speaking Barbey d'Aurevilly did conceive of the
idea that Dandyism should be concerned with the whole man, and
not be confined to the outward dressing of the personality, for he
said that the whole man was not merely what was visible.[19] Yet,
in practice, he does not seem to have considered anything except
the outward manifestations of the Dandy, and it was left to
Baudelaire later to give importance to the inner and hidden
qualities of Dandyism. For him it was chiefly a spiritual conception—in the period of his maturity at all events.

The conception of the Dandy in the eighteen-thirties implied
private means and ample leisure; it implied accepting nothing but
the very best, and great expenditure on the mere façade. Barbey
d'Aurevilly tells us that Beau Brummel wore gloves that fitted

close to his hands as if they had been made of damp muslin, and that they needed four experts to make them—three for the hands and one for the thumbs. He cites also, as the perfection of the conception of the Dandy, the example of the Austrian prince who was so anxious to achieve the correct degree of powder for his hair that he had calculated the size and number of rooms in his palace needed for this purpose if they were lined with footmen armed with puffs who dabbed his hair with powder as he passed slowly the length of the rooms between their serried ranks.'[20]

There were some young men however, who had fought in the ranks at the *Bataille d'Hernani,* who revolted just as strongly as did the Dandies against existing conditions, against prevailing materialism and current bad taste. They did not wish to accept these conditions, yet they were too poor to attempt to make their lives the exquisite achievements that those of the Dandies were. They wished however to protest in their own way, to separate themselves from the masses in their own way; to 'épater le bourgeois' in their own manner and to express their own brand of extravagance. For instance the university students formed themselves into a society called *Les Badouillards* which tried to emulate the Dandies in its own way. It drew up regulations for membership of its association, and aspirants had to go through an ordeal of initiation and a vigil like those which preceded the election of a Knight in the Middle Ages. All members had to be proficient at fencing and boxing, and had to give proof of great physical strength and fitness. They were obliged to give authenticated evidence of courage in various battles. They had moreover to be able to endure all through a night the strenuous dancing of the age. They must be prepared to swear vengeance on the bourgeoisie, to have a repertory of obscene and dangerous political songs with which to disturb the peace and sleep of the common bourgeois. And finally they were not elected until they had performed their night of vigil, which consisted of a Gargantuan meal lasting until midnight, washed down by copious draughts of Champagne, punch, and liqueurs; this was followed by an all night ball where they had to perform everything that they were asked to do and, as the regulations state, to 'engueuler tous ceux qui se présentent devant eux la parole à la bouche, la blague aux lèvres'. Even morning did not bring respite to the candidate for he was obliged to spend the whole of the following day and night going from café to café in fancy dress and to drink all that was put before him. Then, on the third day, if he had not fallen under the table drunk or asleep, he was pronounced 'dignus est intrare' into the company of the *Badouillards*. Probably only the money-lenders knew how much his initiation had cost him.[21]

More important however than the *Badouillards* were the young men of the *Petit Cénacle* who were now to become the *Jeunes France* and very soon later the *Bouzingos*. Though very poor they had many of the ideals of the Dandies—the same scorn of the bourgeoisie, the same hatred of materialism—and they banded themselves into a new gang with Petrus Borel as their leader.

Part Three

THE LYCANTHROPE

Chapter 1

LES BOUZINGOS

In 1831 Petrus Borel and his followers migrated from the Latin Quarter to the heights of Rochechouart—now Boulevard Rochechouart—to imitate Saint Simon who had settled with his own disciples on the hill of Ménilmontant. As he could not afford a whole house, he rented a large room opening on to a garden, at the corner of the Rue d'Auvergne, and called his settlement 'Le Camp des Tartares'. Its members were the former *Petit Cénacle*—Célestin Nanteuil, Bouchardy, Jehan du Seigneur, Philothée O'Neddy, Gérard de Nerval and Théophile Gautier. They were soon however to change their name to *Les Jeunes France*, intending to indicate that they were the youngest, most advanced and most adventurous spirits in France. They declared that they were pledged to fight against philistinism in all its aspects, and against the new order of Louis Philippe. Gautier has given us a description of the headquarters of the association.[1] Since the *Tartares* were poor their room was only scantily furnished—especially in the matter of chairs—so most of the guests were obliged to sit on the floor. But the absence of furniture was redeemed by the originality of the decorations. Devéria and Boulanger had embellished the walls with mural paintings, and Jehan du Seigneur had contributed sculptured medallions; on the mantelpiece stood two antique and very precious Rouen vases, always filled with flowers, and they flanked a grinning skull which took the place of the customary clock in the centre—some part of a human skeleton was an essential accessory for every *Tartare*. It was at this time that Gérard de Nerval, at a dinner at the restaur-

89

ant of Le Petit Moulin Rouge, produced a skull for use as a drinking vessel, claiming that it was that of his father killed at the Battle of the Beresina—he was, as it happened, very much alive and flourishing at the time. When this strange goblet was produced Célestin Nanteuil called out to the waiter: 'Bring us some sea water.' Théophile Gautier asked in astonishment the wherefore of this order and he answered 'Don't you remember that Hugo, in *Han d'Islande*, made his hero drink sea water from the skulls of the dead? Let us follow his example. Garçon une eau de mer!'[2]

On the heights of Rochechouart Borel and his band of *Tartares* followed the nudist teaching of the *Évadistes* and sat in their garden in the summer without any clothes, but they were not left in peace to enjoy their cult, for the neighbours complained to the police that they could see them from their windows, and they were then forbidden, under threat of arrest, from continuing this 'outrage aux mœurs'.[3] They however found other ways of being a source of annoyance and scandal to their neighbours. Sometimes they would drape a dressmaker's dummy which they possessed in a shroud and fling it into the street saying that it was a corpse which they had dug up in the nearby cemetery. At other times they gave concerts in their garden, with a band consisting solely of brass wind at which none of them was proficient so that the result was cacophony.[4] They were constantly in clash with the police who did not at all know how to deal with them. One evening, after they had eaten and drunk too well, they were charging, arm in arm, down the hill towards the city, and shouting lustily to acclaim one of their number: 'Vive Bouchardy! Vive Bouchardy!' This was less than a year after the July Revolution and the crowd thought that they were shouting: 'Vive Charles X! Vive Charles X!' and tried to silence them. The *Jeunes France* defended themselves vigorously and the police rushed forward to quell what they thought was another riot—there had been many since Louis Philippe had seized power—and Gérard de Nerval, the mildest and most inoffensive of the band, but also the easiest to apprehend, was marched off as the ring-leader to prison where he was incarcerated for a month. He has given an account of this experience in *Saint Pélagie*.

The behaviour of the *Jeunes France* eventually wore down the patience of their neighbours and the landlord gave them notice. Then Petrus Borel rented a tiny house consisting of one floor and a basement in a street in the Latin Quarter most appropriately called La Rue d'Enfer—perhaps indeed that was why he chose it— and there he gave one of the most notorious parties of the age as a house-warming—a parody of Dumas' famous fancy-dress party. Ice-cream and custards were served in skulls and the punch was so strong that many of the guests succumbed to its effects and were carried down to the basement which was used as an improvised casualty station, where they were left lying on the floor to recover. Musard's new *Galop Infernal* was danced that evening and since the room was too small for its wild career the front doors were opened and it finished in the street outside.

When the festivities were over Petrus Borel was dubbed 'Prince des audaces et maître suprême des étonnements'.

In the Rue d'Enfer the *Jeunes France* persisted in their notorious behaviour of shocking the public and calling attention to themselves in every possible way. Well known are Gérard de Nerval's perambulations in the Tuileries Gardens with a lobster on a pale blue lead, when he used to say that crustacea pleased his reflective turn of mind, for they do not bite like a dog, nor chatter like children when he wished to meditate. He used also to pitch a tent in the middle of his room and live inside like a primitive man from the bush; or else he would take a large Renaissance bed with him when he went to visit his friends and then, so greatly did he respect it, would sleep beside it on the floor as its devoted slave.

For a time the *Jeunes France* continued to attend Nodier's Sunday literary evenings at the Bibliothèque de L'Arsenal, but they scandalised the more respectable elderly members of this gathering so much by their noisy behaviour and the extravagance of their dress—Gautier came in his red doublet of *Hernani* fame and Borel wore the waistcoat which he alleged was the colour of Polish blood, and his hat with the torrent of motley ribbons flowing down his back. The older men protested to Nodier who explained to the *Jeunes France* that they were a cause of offence, and henceforth they ceased to attend.

Philothée O'Neddy has given a good picture of the wildness and eccentricity of the group in his poem *Pandaemonium* from his collection, *Feu et Flamme*.

> *Et jusques au matin, les damnés Jeunes Frances*
> *Nagèrent dans un flux d'indicibles démences,*
> *—Echangeant leurs poignards—promettant de percer*
> *L'abdomen des chiffreurs—jurant de dépenser*
> *Leur âme à guerroyer contre le siècle aride.—*
> *Tous, les crins vagabonds, l'œil sauvage et torride,*
> *Pareils à des chevaux sans mors ni cavaliers,*
> *Tous hurlant et dansant dans le fauve atelier,*
> *Ainsi que des pensers d'audaces et d'ironie*
> *Dans le crâne orageux d'un homme de génie!*[5]

Soon after settling in the Rue d'Enfer, Borel's followers ceased calling themselves *Les Jeunes France* and adopted the name of *Bouzingos*. The epithet had been hurled at them as a term of abuse but they had picked it up joyfully and wore it with pride. One evening, during one of their frequent clashes with the police, they had been singing loudly as they cavorted through the streets a song whose chorus ran: 'Nous allons faire du bouzingo, du bouzingo, du bouzingo!'[6] Those who heard them began calling them contemptuously 'les bouzingos',* but they pretended to be pleased at this distinction, and adopted the name proudly, saying that henceforth they would be known by no other. They even planned to bring out a joint collection of short stories under the title *Contes du Bouzingo*, but only Gérard de Nerval ever carried out the project and his tale, *Main de Gloire, Conte du Bouzingo*, was published separately, since there was no collection, in the *Cabinet de Lecture* in September 1832. Soon the word *Bouzingo* came to mean anything that was noisy, undisciplined and extravagant. There was even published in *Le Figaro* a satiric biography under the title *Biographie du Bouzingot*. The final 't' should however not have been added as is clear from Philothée O'Neddy's letter on the subject.[7] The number and extent of the articles which appeared for a year in the *Figaro* indicate the notoriety of the *Jeunes France* and

* Bouzingo from 'bousin' meaning a noise.

Bouzingos during the early eighteen-thirties. They occupied almost all the available space in the paper. Between August and October 1831 seven articles were devoted to the *Jeunes France* and, when they had taken the name of *Bouzingos*, between January and June 1832, there were twenty articles and frequent allusions to them. All these contributions were in a satiric vein but they were not at all exaggerated. According to them the houses of the *Bouzingos* are extraordinary for their walls are covered with weapons of every description. One sees notices which say 'Do not touch, this is a poisoned dagger!' or else 'a poisoned arrow'. Or else it is a wolf-trap, a poisoned shirt, a tomahawk, or the scalp of a native chief. The chances are that on the mantelpiece there stands a bowl in which the foetus of a child is preserved in spirit. At dinner, says the *Figaro*, the *Bouzingo* eats wild boar or peacock with its long tail. 'That's right, strong man, eat wild boar, it's indigestible but it's gothic. Peacock is revolting, but it spreads its tail to the sun. Waiter, peacock for four!'

In political opinions the *Bouzingo* is a Republican and against all law and order. He demands liberty, absolute liberty, boundless liberty; liberty to make a row at night and prevent other people from sleeping, liberty to transgress the laws of the land, and to break windows.

The mildest *Bouzingo*, says the *Figaro*, is incapable of writing the shortest note without speaking of death and damnation. He drinks punch from the skull of a dearly loved mistress and stirs the beverage with the shin-bone of a close friend who has died young. He takes his pleasures sadly. 'Sa gaieté est putride' says one of the articles. His favourite pastime is to spend the day in the catacombs, in a cemetery or in a dissecting room. To his lady-love he says, as he shows her a bone, 'You are like this under your ribbons, silks and laces. You walk linked to a skeleton, hugging death close to your heart.'

Yet he is wise to behave thus for all modern girls fall in love with the *Bouzingo*. Their hearts flutter at the sight of the Byronic and 'fatal' lover whom Fate has destined for them. 'See, my sister, how beautiful he is in poetic pallor,' cries one of them, 'how interesting he is! He has Satan's eyes. I love Satan!'

The best and most vivid picture of the *Jeunes France* and *Bouzingos* is the fictional account given by Théophile Gautier in a collection of sketches which he published under the title of *Les Jeunes France*. They were written satirically at a later date when he himself had outgrown the extravagance of his youth. In the main story in the collection, *Daniel Jovard*, we see the hero progressing from normality to extravagance, and it gives a vivid picture of the behaviour of advanced literary young men during the years which followed the Revolution of 1830. At first Daniel is a conventional and old-fashioned young man but he is converted by his close friend, Ferdinand de C., to more progressive views. We are introduced to Ferdinand sitting in his rooms; they are furnished with renaissance pieces, eastern china, strange weapons and fantastic pictures representing scenes of witches' sabbath; there are as well many objects whose use is impossible to imagine—hookahs and other implements for smoking. In the midst of these Ferdinand is seated, wearing a dressing-gown ornamented with dragons, with embroidered slippers on his feet which rest so high on the mantelpiece that he is almost sitting on his head, and he is nonchalantly smoking a Spanish cigarette. He is horrified to discover that Daniel has never smoked and does not know how to dress. He undertakes his education and teaches him how to assume a mediaeval air in order to give himself personality. He makes him throw away his respectable clothes, and orders for him a red waistcoat and a coloured coat. He also makes him grow a long beard and learn by rote anatomical terms so that he could with facility 'parler cadavre'. When we read the dialogue in the writings of Borel, O'Neddy and Janin, we realise how little Gautier has had to exaggerate in order to make his hero ridiculous. After his lessons Jovard is able to write:

> *Par l'enfer! je me sens un immense désir*
> *De broyer sous mes dents sa chair, et de saisir,*
> *Avec quelque lambeau de sa peau blanche et verte,*
> *Son cœur demi-pourri dans sa poitrine ouverte.*[8]

His first task, when emancipated, was to find a suitable name since his own was too common and would not look well as the signature to a sonnet or a picture. After six months of labour he managed to concoct one. The Christian name ended in 'us' and the surname had so many 'k's and 'w's that it was impossible to pronounce.

Having adopted his name he thought of how to make it famous and of selecting an art in which he would shine. At first he decided on painting and produced pictures which were very advanced in the eighteen-thirties but which today might please modern schools of art. His best picture was one of a man with a tiny face partially covered by a long beard, with an abnormally high forehead—that was fashionable in advanced circles and Daniel shaved his in order to make it seem exceptionally high—very little hair and eyebrows meeting below his eyes as was customary amongst Byronic heroes.

Fame however did not come quickly and he deliberated for many weeks on whether he should commit suicide so that his name should appear in the papers. At last he read the press report of the trial and death sentence of a man accused of murder and he then considered assassinating someone so that he could reach fame by being publicly guillotined.

In another story, *Celle-ci et celle-là*, Gautier wrote of a young man called Rodolphe who decided that his next mistress should be as green as an unripe lemon, that her eyebrows should be artifically raised so as to give her a permanently surprised look. Her eyes were to be veiled with eastern melancholy, her nose Jewish, and her hair to be of the same green hue as her face. Rodolphe, like Baudelaire after him, had a passion for cats and he always had several of different sizes and breeds, who used to come and lie in bed with him. He loved them better than anything else in the world—more even than his mistresses.

Rodolphe however ended tragically. One day hearing the bell ring he went down to open the door and in his hurry forgot to remove his nightcap, the badge of the bourgeois, to find his mistress waiting to be admitted. His pride could not survive such a disgrace and shortly afterwards he threw himself into the Seine, reflecting, as he sank to his death, that he would make a beautiful corpse.

Chapter 2

RHAPSODIES

————————————

R*hapsodies*, Borel's first book, appeared in December
1831, although it is dated 1832—the printers worked
more quickly than had been anticipated. It consists of
thirty-four poems written mostly when he was twenty
and twenty-one. The quotation from Malherbe which figures on
the title page is very typical of Borel's truculence, of his pose of
despising approbation, of his contempt for the critic.

> *Vous dont les censures s'étendent*
> *Dessus les ouvrages de tous,*
> *Ce livre se moque de vous,*[1]

Borel's professed intention in writing this book is to astound
his readers and to make them, willy nilly, conscious of his bitterness and feeling of revolt. He sets forth his aims in a mordant and
uncompromising preface written in 1831. The poems which follow
are to be the 'scories', that is to say the 'slag' of his nature. He
starts without any preliminaries, in order to attract attention.[2]
'A child must discharge its dribble before being able to speak
frankly; the poet must also discharge his; I have discharged mine:
here it is! The metal seething in the melting-pot must discharge
its slag; the poetry seething in my breast has its own. Here it is!
And so these Rhapsodies are scum and slag. Yes!'

The poems then are intended to show Borel as he really is,
without any disguise, and let his readers like him or dislike him
according to their will, but at least they will know him. The book
is himself, he did not write it, it wrote itself. With pride and

arrogance he declares that he has never been the disciple of anyone, and that this explains why he is poor and unknown. Instead
of appealing for the support of rich and powerful patrons, of those
who could help him, he dedicates his book to his followers and
friends, the *Bouzingos* as poor and as unknown as he, comrades in
adversity—Jehan du Seigneur, Bouchardy, Brot and O'Neddy. In
the Preface he mentions for the first time his lycanthropy, his
violent republicanism and love of liberty. 'I am a republican in the
way a lynx might be. My republicanism is lycanthropy.' The
Preface ends on a truculent and cynical note. He says that luckily
we have, to console us for our bad government, adultery and
tobacco.

The most original and typical qualities of Petrus Borel are to be
found in this Preface and he did not progress any further. Indeed
he never completely fulfilled its promise. A few years later, in the
Preface to *Champavert*, he wrote, referring to *Rhapsodies*, 'Never
did a publication create a greater scandal, the sort of scandal
which will always be caused by a book written with the heart and
soul, without any consideration for our age. The book was
impregnated with gall and suffering.'[3]

When he wrote this passage Borel was thinking of what he had
intended to do and not of what he had actually achieved. The
poems themselves are not, except in a few cases, an intimate
record, nor an expression of personal suffering. They are too far
from being the scum or the slag of a passionate and unruly nature
to fulfil the promise of the Preface. It was original to set forth such
a daring conception of poetry but *Rhapsodies* does not entirely carry
out its truculent claims. The explanation for this may be that the
Preface was written after the poems and that it expresses the
bitterness and revolt which Borel felt as a result of the Revolution; the poems, on the contrary, were written, for the greater
part, much earlier and in a less disturbed atmosphere. Most of them
are gentle and sentimental in character, not vastly different from the
bulk of poetry produced in the early years of the Romantic
Movement.

After the Preface comes the Prologue which sets forth his
gratitude to the architect Clopet who had given him shelter

when he was destitute. It expresses no more than this and the reader wonders why it should be called a Prologue. Of the poems that follow it, some are mildly emotional, very similar in inspiration to the poems found in *Keepsakes* fashionable in the early Romantic period—these elegant little books printed on pale blue or pale pink paper, delightfully illustrated and exquisitely bound, fit gifts for society ladies. *Larmes à mon Frère Benoni* is a sentimental poem in the vein of Marceline Desbordes Valmore, in memory of a brother who had died young after a delicate youth. It expresses the hope that he, who had known so little rest during his short life, should be allowed to sleep in peace. There are other poems very suitable for Romantic collections. Poems such as *Le Médaillon d'Iseult* and *Isolement* in which he dreams of a nymph with blue eyes and golden hair who will become his love. These come strangely from the pen of the poet who prided himself on having experienced the throes of a devouring passion. Even when he does write of passionate love it recalls the licence of a Bertin in the eighteenth-century rather than passion as Baudelaire was later to understand it. Such a poem is *Victoire*. *Le Rendez-Vous*, however, stands out amongst these mild poems of love in having a hint of the grimness which we shall find in *Champavert*. It tells of a lover waiting for his mistress to come and reviling her because she is late. Eventually she appears but borne along in her coffin. He stabs himself so as to be able to follow her.

One would have imagined, from the Preface, that revolutionary zeal would have inspired Borel, but *Chant du Réveil*, written in December 1830, *La Nuit du 28 au 29* and *Sansculottide* composed in 1831, have nothing revolutionary but their titles. They express conventional emotions in pedestrian language. Political fervour was certainly not for Borel a vital source of literary emotion. His invective is far below that of Barbier in his *Iambes* published in 1830.

There are in *Rhapsodies* however poems which give Borel the right to an individual and permanent place in French poetry. The most original in the collection are *Désespoir*, *Hymne au Soleil*, *Heur et Malheur* and *Misère*. *Hymne au Soleil* is a poem which Baudelaire might have written and it has a realism of expression which was hitherto met only in certain poems of *Les Poésies de Joseph Delorme* of Sainte-Beuve. In 1830, when mediaeval castles and landscapes were fashionable, few thought of looking at the material world around them. Balzac had not yet published his novels which gave the public a taste for sordid realism. Borel here describes the sun as shining down on all the hunger, filth and exploitation of a modern city, shining on them all with equal impartiality. *Heur et Malheur* is an expression of genuine personal feeling and we find in it the same idea as in Baudelaire's *Bénédiction*, the conception of the cursed nature of the poet. It is very different from the noble pride of Vigny in his fate as a writer to be 'puissant et solitaire'. Borel shows the poet as the prey of poverty, suffering and despair. The poem is prophetic of his own future career.

The collection ends with *Misère* which is a worthy epilogue; it would also serve as an epilogue to Borel's unfortunate life. He declares that he feels inspiration rising in him but that he is fettered and bound down to earth by poverty and lack of sympathy and understanding. The poem is amongst his most successful and heartfelt. It ends.

> *Que de fois, sur le roc qui borde cette vie,*
> *Ai-je frappé du pied, heurté du front l'envie,*
> *Criant contre le ciel mes longs tourmens soufferts:*
> *Je sentais ma puissance, et je sentais des fers!*
> *Puissance . . . fers . . . quoi donc?—rien, encore un poète*
> *Qui ferait du divin, mais sa muse est muette,*
> *Sa puissance est aux fers.—Allons! on ne croit plus,*
> *En ce siècle voyant, qu'aux talens révolus.*
> *Travaille, on ne croit plus aux futures merveilles,*
> *Travaille! . . . Eh! le besoin qui me hurle aux oreilles,*
> *Étouffant tout penser qui se dresse en mon sein!*
> *Aux accords de mon luth que répondre? . . . j'ai faim!*[4]

Yet it was not poverty alone that fettered Borel, but a certain limitation in his creative powers and in his talent. He knew what poetry could and should be; he felt it in his heart and knew it intellectually, but there was some barrier between his inspiration and his expression; the soil was not sufficiently fertile for the seed, and it only occasionally came to full fruition. His tragedy was one not uncommon amongst men of talent and sensitivity; his creative ability did not match his vision and his ambition.

In *Rhapsodies* Borel's most fruitful source of inspiration was his own poverty and lack of recognition, and there are few spiritual dreams or visions in his poems, for he rarely goes beyond personal hunger and distress. This was probably responsible for his lack of success amongst his contemporaries and for the fact that posterity did not single him out for a high place amongst the immortals, in spite of his gifts. Béranger sensed this flaw in Borel's art when he received a copy of *Rhapsodies*. He realised that Borel's diatribes against the social order were inspired by his own suffering rather than by a wider human compassion and conviction. 'I too have been young and melancholy like you' he wrote to Borel in an appreciative letter which showed intuitive understanding, 'and like you I have attacked the social order on the score of my own suffering and distress. When I was young I composed odes in which I gave expression to the resolve to go and live amongst the wolves.' He went on to say that hardships do not last eternally and advised him to stick to his writing, not to lose hope and courage, and not to show his bleeding wounds to the world.

Rhapsodies did not create any stir when it appeared. Only one periodical deigned to review it—*La Revue Encyclopédique* in November 1831. In the Preface to *Champavert* Borel mentions a second edition but no traces of this have been found, though certainly some copies exist with the words 'Second Edition' printed on the title page, but these seem only to be the same printing of the 1831 edition to which a new title page and frontispiece have been added. This is a frequent practice amongst French publishers.

Although *Rhapsodies* did not bring its author wide fame or wealth he could at least take pride in having had a 'succès d'estime'. He consoled himself with the thought that masterpieces do not immediately impress themselves on the public—his friends confirmed him in this belief. He thought that he was now sufficiently well known to found his own paper which should express his ideals and those of his followers, those whom he called the lion-hearted *Jeunes France*. In 1832 they returned to their former name of *Jeunes France* and dropped the one of *Bouzingos*. In 1832, when he had scraped together sufficient capital, Borel started a periodical called *La Liberté, Journal des Arts*.[5] Its aim was to attack all established institutions like the University, the Schools and the Academy; also classical art in all its forms, in painting, sculpture, architecture, music and poetry. The magazine was to deal with all the arts on an equal footing and the specialised articles were entrusted to various artists. Jehan du Seigneur dealt with sculpture and Delacroix wrote on painting.

The first number appeared in September 1832 and Borel wrote an inflammatory leading article which he signed with a pseudonym. 'It is said that a prospectus recently announced that a group of dedicated young men, united by one single ideal, feeling cramped in our bastard régime, and stifled by the Academy, the Schools and the University, had banded themselves together to win for their brothers the same liberty which they had won for themselves by the force of their own arms, at their own risk. This manifesto—for it is indeed a war we are waging and which must be fought to a finish—appeals to all artists, architects, engravers, painters, musicians, and poets. Now this voice that has spoken has been heard on all sides and echoes of it have reached us from all quarters. Everything that is generous in France responds—from the Schools, the studios, from the gates of the Academy itself, almost from its precincts—they have rushed forward in crowds, in serried ranks, full of dash and courage, men demanding a leader and orders to fulfil. The seed has produced a harvest: the nut has grown into a tree; isolated individuals have become a crowd; the army is ready, the soldiers are trained and the orders which hitherto have only been whispered, are now shouted in a loud voice. Death to the Academy! Death to the Schools! Death to the University! We shall throw down our arms only when we have built for the Académie des Beaux Arts a grave with stones torn from the Palais des Quatre Nations.[6] Did you not believe that we would be able to bury in oblivion a few old men and gag a few toothless mouths. We young men hope for better things!

Is that not true, young men? So cheer in a loud voice all of you, for the future is beautiful!'[7]

As long as the magazine lasted Borel enjoyed a modicum of fame and success, certainly amongst his contemporaries. They kept on telling him that he was the great man of his age, the leader of youth; they told him that he would soon surpass even Hugo and take his place. At this time Hugo had begun to disappoint his early followers. He had by now thrown aside his liberal opinions and had accepted Louis Philippe, he was even soon to become a close friend of the heir apparent, the Duke of Orleans. He was considered by all the younger men, who had given him their support at the moment of *Hernani*, to have let them down, for he was now seeking only popular success, and producing dramas which were pure melodrama and not to be distinguished from those of Pixérécourt. And, most reprehensible of all, he was now making large sums of money from his writings and becoming as materialistic as any bourgeois.

Borel now had a few years of popularity and fame. He was full of bright hopes for the future, full also of pathetic pride and arrogance. He was less flamboyant than he had been in the days of his house-warming at the Rue d'Enfer. His pose was now one of sombre dignity. He usually wore the clothes in which he is seen in the portrait by Boulanger—his best portrait—the severe black tailed-coat, buttoned up to the neck and showing only the narrowest rim of white; the close-fitting black trousers, and the shiny patent-leather boots. In the portrait we see the spaniel whom he loved more deeply than even his closest friends.

At this time he was seen at all the literary functions. He was one of the most important and spectacular figures of the day, all the contemporary accounts confirm this. There is no mention of any important gathering at which Petrus Borel was not a striking and an honoured guest.

Chapter 3

FEU ET FLAMME

T wo years after the publication of *Rhapsodies* there appeared a collection of poems called *Feu et Flamme* by Philothée O'Neddy, which carried out more fully than Petrus Borel had done, the ideas of his provocative Preface to *Rhapsodies*. *Feu et Flamme* is the most violent work produced by the *Bouzingo* poets; these poems are indeed the scum and the slag of their author. They are the explosion of a young writer who has not yet learnt discipline. O'Neddy, far more than Borel, had 'broyé du fer rouge', and yet he never enjoyed the fame and notoriety of the Lycanthrope. Perhaps this was because his personality was less flamboyantly picturesque and he had not the same pride and arrogance. The young take their contemporaries at their own valuation, and Borel's valuation of himself was high.

Who then was Philothée O'Neddy who appeared for so short a time as a star on the horizon of poetry and then faded away so quickly?

Philothée O'Neddy, who, as we have already seen, began life with the more ordinary name of Théophile Dondey, was born in Paris on 30 January 1811. His father was a minor civil servant, employed at the Ministry of Finance, and although his family was not rich, young Dondey suffered no hardships in his youth. While still a boy at the famous Lycée Louis-le-Grand he came under the influence of the magazine called *Le Globe*, a paper whose republican and liberal views attracted the younger and more progressive writers between 1824, when it was founded, and 1830.

On leaving school O'Neddy gravitated to *Le Petit Cénacle* and became one of the planets revolving around Petrus Borel. Like his friends and contemporaries he fought at the *Bataille d'Hernani* and was carried away by enthusiasm for the Revolution of 1830. Like them also he was bitterly disappointed with the results of the revolt and was left with the same desire for destruction.

Gautier has given us, in his *Histoire du Romantisme*, a vivid portrait of O'Neddy at the time of the *Les Bouzingos*. He was so dark skinned as to seem almost like a mulatto, but, as a violent contrast, he had thick fair woolly hair and extraordinarily blue eyes, very beautiful eyes, made more dreamy and mysterious by their astigmatism. They were so short-sighted as sometimes to appear unseeing, and he used to say that he had to keep his glasses on at night when he went to bed in order to be able to see his dreams. The general impression that he gave was that of a fair Moor, and his friends used to call him 'the blond Othello'.

O'Neddy wrote the poems published under the title *Feu et Flamme* in 1829 and 1830, but they were not printed until 1833 though the collection was ready at the time of the Revolution. He lost his father in the terrible cholera epidemic of the spring of 1832, and with him the small modicum of financial security he had hitherto enjoyed. This put an end to his plans for becoming a man of letters. His father died after twenty-nine years of service when he was on the point of retiring but, since he had died before actually reaching retiring age, his widow received no pension. O'Neddy was then left as sole support of his widowed mother and unmarried sister. He did not shrink from shouldering the burden and he became a civil servant as his father had been. The Ministry of Finance appointed him to the same post and he held it until he himself reached retiring age.

His literary friends were disappointed in him and dropped him. They may have thought it unworthy of a *Bouzingo*, unworthy of the creator of *Feu et Flamme*, to settle down so quickly; and, to be moved by the bourgeois virtue of a sense of responsibility towards his family, would have seemed to them incomprehensible and contemptible.

He was now a civil servant in a black suit, with a stiff collar and neat tie. He determined however to publish the poems which he

PHILOTHÉE O'NEDDY
From a photograph

had composed when he was eighteen and nineteen. Perhaps he thought that their fame might later permit him to rely solely on his writings for a living. After all Victor Hugo was known to make large sums of money from his poetry and to keep a growing family from it.

The book was printed by his cousin Dondey Dupré, and it appeared in August 1833. It is a very beautiful little book, elegantly printed on good paper, with a frontispiece by Célestin Nanteuil. The edition was limited to three hundred copies and it was paid for by the author himself. Today this slim little volume is considered one of the gems amongst Romantic publications, one of the most eagerly sought after by bibliophiles and treasured when found. It is one of the prettiest books of the time.

The title *Feu et Flamme* was intended to startle and to arouse curiosity, likewise the Preface. 'Like you I despise, from the height of my soul, the social order,' wrote O'Neddy, 'and especially the political order which is its excrement;—like you I do not care a fig for the old fogies and the Academy; like you I stand unmoved and incredulous before the pompous magniloquence and tawdry tinsel finery of the religions of the world; like you I have pious elation towards poetry only, that twin sister of God.'

Daring also are the titles of the separate poems: *Pandæmonium, Nécropolis, Succube, Incantation, Spleen, Névralgie* and so forth. Borel's titles in *Rhapsodies* seem mild and innocent in comparison. Yet, in spite of this, the book aroused little interest. Its fire and flame spluttered out without leaving sufficient light to illuminate the name of its author, and he sank down into obscurity and oblivion in his government office.

La Revue Encyclopédique paid him the honour of attacking him on the score of his offensiveness to standard art and conventional morality. The critic raised his voice in protest against the empty and dangerous ideas which he claimed were being propagated in certain quarters on the plea of the freedom of poetry.

O'Neddy tried to secure the support of Chateaubriand by sending him a copy of his book. But the 'father of Romanticism', now a saddened and ageing man, was horrified at the violence and extravagance of this unknown descendant of his René. He had now grown old and he preached to his children. He told his young follower not to profane the great gifts which Heaven had bestowed on him and to respect Christianity and tradition.

The strongest impression that is conveyed by *Feu et Flamme* is one of anguish and distress, which will not be met to such an extent until the poetry of Baudelaire. The poems contain a bitterness and a *spleen* that surpasses anything in those of Borel. Baudelaire, as a young man, may have modelled his personality largely on that of the *lycanthrope*, but it is from *Feu et Flamme* rather than from *Rhapsodies* that he drew the substance of his first manner. In his critical writings the name of Philothée O'Neddy is not mentioned, nor has he ever referred to *Feu et Flamme*. Perhaps this may have been because he never had occasion to do so. It was the death of Petrus Borel in 1859 that gave him the pretext for his article on him which was published in *La Revue Fantaisiste*. O'Neddy, at the time of Baudelaire's death, was still vegetating in his government office, forgotten by everybody. Yet the similarity of some of Baudelaire's poetry to that of O'Neddy is remarkable; there are lines and turns of phrase that are sometimes almost identical in both poets. 'Le terrible jamais vibre comme un tocsin' from *Névralgie* in *Feu et Flamme* is a line that Baudelaire might have written; while the following from O'Neddy's *Nécropolis*:

> Plus de rages d'amour! le cœur stagnant et morne
> Ne se sent plus broyé sous la dent du remords.

is reminiscent of Baudelaire's *Irréparable*:

> l'Irréparable ronge avec sa dent maudite
> Notre âme, piteux monument.

While a further couplet from *Nécropolis*:

> Ose à la fois être le juge,
> La victime et l'exécuteur.

is like one from *L'Héautontimorouménos* by Baudelaire:

> Je suis les membres et la roue,
> Et la victime et le bourreau!

And was it in the lines from *Amour* of *Feu et Flamme*, 'Puis-je assez te chérir, mon ange, mon idole?' and further:

> *Mets tes yeux sur mes yeux. Donne à ma lèvre, donne,*
> *Ta lèvre séraphique, ô ma blanche Madone!*

that Baudelaire found his own lines 'Je suis l'Ange gardien, la Muse, la Madone' and also:

> *A l'Ange, à l'idole immortelle,*
> *Salut en l'immortalité.*

At eighteen Philothée O'Neddy expresses the same *ennui* that Baudelaire was to express twenty years later at twenty-five, and his efforts compare favourably with those of his older and more famous successor. He writes in a poem called *Spleen*.

> *Oh! combien de mes jours le cercle monotone*
> *Effare ma pensée et d'ennuis la couronne!*
> *Que faire de mon âme et de ses saints transports,*
> *Dans cet air étouffant qui pèse sur la ville,*
> *Au milieu d'une foule insouciante et vile,*
> *Où dort l'enthousiasme, où tous les cœurs sont morts!*

This is very like one of the *Spleen* poems by Baudelaire, not to mention the 'des mortels la multitude vile' from *Recueillement*.

There is in O'Neddy a love of Satanism and the occult, an affection for love potions, for pacts with the devil, for necromancy, which recall Baudelaire's interests when he was young. O'Neddy writes in *Rodomontade*:

> *Non, non! Je creuserais les sciences occultes;*
> *Je m'en irais, la nuit, par des sites incultes,*
> *Et là, me raillant du Seigneur,*
> *Je tourbillonnerais dans la magie infâme,*
> *J'évoquerais le Diable . . . et je vendrais mon âme*
> *Pour quelque mille ans de bonheur.*

We find also in him the blending of good and evil, the contrast between *spleen* and *idéal* which is so characteristic a feature of

Baudelaire's work. The following lines from *Delta* might have been written by Baudelaire in his youth:

> *C'est qu'à la fois je tiens du démon et de l'ange:*
> *C'est que, par un caprice intraduisible, étrange,*
> *—Que tu concevras toi,*
> *Mais qui susciterait des sots la pitié grave,—*
> *Je veux être à la fois ton maître et ton esclave,*
> *Ton vassal et ton roi!*

Love for O'Neddy was the same torture and battle that it was to be for Baudelaire, and *Eros* from *Feu et Flamme* strikes a strange note in the midst of the sentimental effusions of 1829. *Amour* is even truly Baudelairean in style and inspiration.

> *Laisse, fée aux yeux noirs, laisse mon corps jaloux,*
> *Comme un serpent lascif, s'étendre à tes genoux!*
> *Lorsque la vénusté de son éclat m'obombre,*
> *Dieu seul de mes bonheurs pourrait dire le nombre.*
> *Laisse ma tête en feu se serrant contre toi,*
> *Caresser follement ta robe; laisse-moi*
> *Sous l'amour de tes yeux qui me trempent de flamme,*
> *Respirer, comme un vague et saisissant dictame,*
> *Que je boive à pleins bords l'oubli des mauvais jours!*
> *Ma reine, dis-moi bien que tu seras toujours,*
> *Dans les sables brûlans de ma vie agitée,*
> *Mon ombreuse oasis et ma coupe enchantée.*

Only the third and fourth lines would seem too clumsy for a poem by Baudelaire. But the image of the lover compared to a serpent, or a cluster or worms, is a favourite one with him; so too is the description of the opiate powers of his mistress's perfume. There are lines here that recall *Le Léthé* and *La Chevelure* by Baudelaire.

For a final example of O'Neddy's talent and inspiration there is *Succube* which contains a whole nosegay of *Fleurs du Mal*.

> *Je rêvais, l'autre nuit, qu'aux splendeurs des orages,*
> *Sur le parquet mouvant d'un salon de nuages,*

De terreur et d'amour puissamment tourmenté,
Avec une lascive et svelte Bohémienne,
　　　Dans une valse aérienne,
　　　Ivre et fou j'étais emporté.

Comme mon bras cerclait sa taille fantastique!
D'un sein que le velours comprimait élastique
Oh! comme j'aspirais les irritans parfums!
Et que j'étais heureux, lorsque, brusque et sauvage,
　　　Le vent roulait sur mon visage
　　　Les gerbes de ses cheveux bruns!

Un fou rire la prit . . . rire désharmonique,
Digne de s'éployer au banquet satanique.
J'eus le frisson, mes dents jetèrent des strideurs.—
Puis, soudain, plus de fée à lubrique toilette!
　　　Plus rien dans mes bras qu'un squelette
　　　M'étalant toutes ses hideurs!

Oh! comme en ton amour se complaît ta valseuse!
Murmurait sa voix rauque. Et sa poitrine osseuse
Pantelait de désir, râlait de volupté.
Et puis toujours, toujours, de nuage en nuage,
　　　Avec elle au fort de l'orage,
　　　Je bondissais épouvanté!

Pour me débarrasser de sa luxure avide,
Je luttais vainement dans la brume livide.
De ses bras anguleux l'enlacement profond
S'incrustait dans mes chairs ruisselantes de fièvre,
　　　Et les baisers aigus de sa bouche sans lèvre
　　　M'incisaient la joue et le front.

Amongst lines that are reminiscent of various poems from *Les Fleurs du Mal* there are certain which Baudelaire would never have written. As a whole the poem is very similar in inspiration to his *Métamorphoses du Vampire*.

It is not intended to exaggerate the debt that Baudelaire may owe to the poems of Philothée O'Neddy. *Feu et Flamme* is like work written by a young and inexperienced Baudelaire—not that clumsiness is always absent even from Baudelaire's mature work —but it must not be forgotten that O'Neddy was only eighteen and nineteen when he composed the poems and that they are considerably superior to those which we have from Baudelaire's pen at the same age. If *Feu et Flamme* were signed by Baudelaire we should think it a remarkable achievement for a youth who had only just left school, and we should see in it the seeds of his future genius. The tragedy with O'Neddy was that these poems were not the seed but the full flowering of his talent and the highest point he was to reach. Gautier wrote of him in 1861 in *Le Château du Souvenir.*

> *Celui-ci me conta ses rêves*
> *Hélas! jamais réalisés.*
> *Icare tombé sur les grêves*
> *Où gisent les espoirs brisés.*[1]

Chapter 4

CHAMPAVERT

The notoriety and fame which came from *Rhapsodies* and *La Liberté, Journal des Arts*, did not fill Borel's pockets, and to make a living he was obliged to contribute to any paper, however unsuitable, which would take his work. He, the *Lycanthrope*, the 'broyeur de fer rouge', published poems in the popular romantic *Keepsakes*. It was in the *Annales Romantiques* that *Heur et Malheur* was reprinted in 1832, and the first of his short stories, *Les Pressentimens*, appeared in *l'Album de la Mode, Chronique du Monde Fashionable*; this was a charming collection with illustrations by Tony Johannot. One wonders, however, how the girls, for whom it was intended, enjoyed Borel's grim tale. But this was the year of the cholera and the stomachs of even the youngest maidens were strong.

The tale relates how, at midnight on a certain day every year, Count Jossereau used to gather his family and retainers together to commemorate his wife's death. On the fifth anniversary they had all assembled as usual and were engaged in melancholy conversation, and also singing funeral hymns. At the stroke of midnight a sumptuous meal was served in the very room in which the poor lady had died, a room draped in black for the occasion, with hangings spangled with silver tears, while a coverlet on which was embroidered a white cross lay over the bed, and tall black candles burned at its four corners. The guests were all dressed in deep mourning and, kneeling, recited, as grace before the meal, seven penitential psalms. In this gloomy setting Count Jossereau terrifies his guests still more by relating his premonition that further misfortunes await his family, and recalls similar warnings which have been the prelude to sinister happenings. His daughter, a beautiful girl of twenty, pours scorn on the gloomy superstitions of her father, and scandalises the company by her sacrilegious jokes. After she has played the *Funeral March* of Beethoven— probably Borel is here recalling the occasion when he had heard Liszt play it on a night of the cholera—this tragic music exacerbating still further the nervous tension of the gathering, she declares that she is not frightened, and to prove it she says that she will go to the neighbouring cemetery and gather a sprig of cypress there to show that she has fulfilled her wager. A few moments later she returns carrying over her arm a shroud which she says was thrown over her while she was in the churchyard. She demands who has played her this trick but all disclaim knowledge of the incident, and the shroud, on examination, proves not to belong to the household but to have a large 'S' embroidered in black in one corner—the initial of Satan. The foolhardy girl, now utterly terrified, falls in a dead faint on the ground. A month later she dies and is carried to the cemetery where she had gone to brave the forces of darkness.

La Liberté, Journal des Arts did not prosper and it died six months after its birth, in February 1833, when the small original subsidy was exhausted. Borel did not however allow himself to be down-hearted for he had now, ready for publication, his next book, *Champavert, Contes Immoraux*, and he hoped much from its success. It came out in 1833. It is his most important work and gives a faithful impression of his characteristic qualities: his love of horror relieved by his own brand of grim humour and irony, his talent for vivid narrative. It is also very typical of the age. *Champavert* is Borel's most original work and its appearance is the highest point of his literary career. It was published by Renuel who is famous for having produced so many elegant collections of the writings of the Romantic poets. In claiming that these tales are immoral Borel exaggerates. Some are horrifying, some are cynical and cruel, with touches of the sadism which was fashionable in that period; they all possess his grim ironical humour— 'l'humour noire' as André Breton calls it—but they are not, most of them, particularly immoral; certainly less so than Gautier's *Mademoiselle de Maupin* which was to be published three years later.

The collection opens with a Preface entitled *Notice sur Champavert* which gives an account of the presumed author. It is modelled on the *Vie, Pensées et Poésies de Joseph Delorme* by Sainte-Beuve published in 1829. Sainte-Beuve, wishing to publish a collection of his own poems, pretended that they were the work of a certain Joseph Delorme who had recently died in great poverty and who, if he had not died, would certainly have committed suicide. In telling the story of Delorme's life Sainte-Beuve gives an account of his own and of his early struggles. Petrus Borel adopts the same convention for Champavert and says that he committed suicide and that, after his death, it was discovered that he had earlier published a book of poems called *Rhapsodies* under the pseudonym of Petrus Borel. These *Contes Immoraux* are his second and posthumous work. Borel then gives an account of the life of Champavert, which is his own life as he wants it to be known, and he quotes some poems from *Rhapsodies*, those which he considers most worthy of notice and they are, as it happens, the best. Then, just as Sainte-Beuve had quoted aphorisms by Joseph Delorme in a postscript, Borel quotes some from the pen of Champavert and some of these are reminiscent of Baudelaire's in *Fusées*. For instance he writes: 'Dans Paris il y a deux cavernes, l'une de voleurs et l'autre de meurtriers; celle de voleurs c'est la Bourse, celle de Meurtriers c'est le Palais-de-Justice.'[1]

Champavert is composed of five tales which correspond to what is normally accepted as a short story. These are *Monsieur d'Argentière, Jacquez Barraou, L'Anatomiste, Three Fingered Jack* and *Dina la Belle Juive*. There are two additional narratives which can hardly be called stories. These are *Passereau l'Ecolier* and *Champavert le Lycanthrope*, which are autobiographical sketches—especially the second which is Borel's account of his own life.

The first story, *Monsieur de l'Argentière*, has little that appeals to us nowadays. The style has not much distinction and the psychology is that of the serial novel. It has however some effective descriptive writing which gives a good impression of the Paris of the nineteenth century, and there is a surprising chapter called

Rococo which describes very cleverly a Louis XV dining room. One would not have expected a *Bouzingo* to have had a taste for rococo; its description however suffers somewhat from what will eventually be Borel's besetting sin, a tendency towards pedantry and towards making too great a show of learning.

Monsieur de l'Argentière is the story of a man, the public prosecutor, who taking advantage of a friend's absence, creeps into his fiancée's room at night and, under cover of darkness, seduces her. She, thinking that he is the man to whom she is engaged, yields to him. She becomes pregnant and when her fiancé returns and sees her condition, he refuses to believe her story. He breaks off his engagement with her and leaves her to her fate. Eventually she bears the child, and in a fit of post-confinement madness, alone and without help, she throws the baby down a sewer believing it to be dead. It is found but dies on being picked up. It is traced back to her but she remembers nothing about the event. After a trial she is condemned to death through the offices of the man who has seduced her and whom she recognises in the Court. The story ends with the public execution which the prosecutor watches from his window. But, just at the end, there is a characteristic touch of Borel's bitter irony which saves the tale from triviality. It was raining during the execution and the crowd, not getting a full view of the scaffold, cries: 'Down with your umbrellas, no one can see anything! Down with your umbrellas! And the women repeated 'Behave like gentlemen, no one can see anything!' And Borel ends: 'The rabble, craning their necks, were on tip-toes. When the knife fell a low dull murmur could be heard; and an Englishman, leaning out of a window for which he had paid twenty pounds, cried in a satisfied voice, as he clapped, "Very well!" '[2]

The second story, *Jacquez Barraou*, with its sombre and passionate character, is of a higher standard artistically. It is a well-told story of bitter sexual jealousy, of a fight to a tragic finish for the possession of a girl, ending with the death of both contestants. There is however tenderness and compassion as well as cruelty. In a particularly touching scene the two fighting enemies stop belabouring one another and fall on their knees to say the

Angelus as the church bells ring out. Then, when they have finished praying, they resume the fight. Here too the story ends with a peculiarly Borellian touch. The two negroes have finally killed each other and lie dead, still locked in combat. A white shopkeeper walks by, stumbles against the corpses of the two dead rivals and says, as he passes on unmoved, 'They are only niggers!'

Another tale of negro life is *Three Fingered Jack*—Borel is very successful with these studies of primitive people—where unconscious cruelty, or even sadism, is mingled with tenderness. It is the story of a black Robin Hood called Three Fingered Jack because he has lost two fingers from his right hand in combat. He has, in spite of all his crimes, never yet hurt a woman or a child—indeed he has saved Abigail, the heroine, from being carried away as a slave. In the picture that Borel draws of Three Fingered Jack it is obvious that he is really thinking of himself; he sees himself as a Robin Hood who might flee thus from everyday life, and he says: 'Jack was one of these strong characters, one of these powerful brains, born to rule, who unable to breathe in the narrow cage in which fate has placed them, in that society which wants to bend and to shrink everything to its own mean size, break forever men whom they loathe, if they do not break with life itself. Three Fingered Jack was a lycanthrope.'[3]

There is in this story the same violence and bloodshed as in the others, with a full account of death by knifing. There are also traces of his besetting sin, the excessive parade of erudition which we also found in *Monsieur de l'Argentière*. There is a chapter—he calls it, with justification, *Tiresome Chapter*—in which he gives the sources of his material, taken largely from a *Treatise of Sugar* by a certain Doctor Moseley. The chapter is irrelevant to the story, the material, if given at all, should have figured in a footnote, and it serves no purpose but to display the learning of its author.

L'Anatomiste, exemplifying the grimmest and most macabre side of Borel's talent, is one his most effective tales. It is the story of an old doctor of anatomy, Don Andrea Vesalius, who marries a young beautiful girl and then, after the wedding, finds that, in spite of his great love and passion, he is impotent with her. He

reads her accounts from classical writers to show that the extremes
of love often cause such failure, but he cannot cure himself and
his excuses do not interest his wife. Borel adds ironically: 'Vesalius
once more betrothed himself to learning.'

Vesalius then shuts himself away in his laboratory and gives
himself up more than ever to research. He allows his young wife
to go her own way, but under the vigilance of a duenna who
reports all her doings to him. The young woman diverts herself
by taking young lovers, beautiful young men, who seem to be in
unlimited supply—and her husband apparently does not notice
her behaviour. She expresses little surprise when each lover disappears after one short night of love, even before she has wakened,
and she never sees him again. This does not however worry her
overmuch, as others never fail to appear. After two years of
marriage she falls ill and sends for her husband for she thinks that
she is on the point of death, and she wishes to ease her conscience
by confessing her guilt. She excuses herself on the grounds of her
youth and his age, and begs him to forgive her. He pulls aside her
hands clinging to him, and bids her rise from her bed to follow him
to the laboratory. In that gruesome setting he forces her to listen
to his side of the story. He tells her that he has never been her
dupe, that it was he who had provided her with her lovers, and
that each of them who had slept with her was afterwards drugged
by the duenna through his orders, and later carried down asleep
to the laboratory, to become a specimen for dissection. He then
points to a skeleton hanging in a cupboard on which hang the
clothes of her first lover. Then he shows her, in a glass container,
a human skeleton partially preserved in spirit, the arteries are
filled with a red liquid and the veins with blue, all visible to
observe. The hair and the beard are still on the skull. It is clear that
it is Fernando her second lover. Finally she is shown her last,
Pedro, and at this sight she falls to the ground in a faint. The next
day a coffin is carried out of the palace and the gravedigger
notices that it is very heavy and gives a resonant sound unlike
that of a corpse.

The following evening anyone looking in at Vesalius as he
worked in his laboratory, could have seen him dissecting the

corpse of a beautiful young woman whose long fair hair fell to the ground.

Dina la Belle Juive is a gruesome tale of rape and suicide, which has little unity of plan, though it possesses dramatic tension and vividness of writing. It takes place at Lyons where Borel had lived as a boy, and he has marvellously evoked the atmosphere of the town, with its narrow mediaeval streets down by the river. The opening section of the story might be a scene for light opera, the final chapter would be better told as a ballad, while the centre portion, the account of the rape and sadistic murder of Dina by the boatman whom she has hired to row her across the river, is a separate story fit for *grand guignol*. The story ends with the usual ironic touch characteristic of Borel. The boatman, who has bound and gagged Dina, robbed, raped and murdered her, finally flinging her into the river, fishes her up again next day and tries to claim the reward offered by the Corporation for salvaging drowned corpses. He does not however succeed in his plan for they will not pay for a Jew. 'Who fishes up a heretic, sir boatman, fishes up a dog!'

Passereau l'Ecolier and *Testament de Champavert* are the most interesting and original parts of the collection, they are also the most significant through their influence, especially on Baudelaire. Passereau, the Paris student, could only have been conceived by a morbid mind. He had once believed in women and in love, but he suddenly discovers, from reading, in the absence of his mistress, her letters, that she has another lover as well as him. He entices her to a lonely garden and then drowns her in a well, watching her torments as she tries to escape and finishing her off with stones torn from the rim of the well. Then he goes to her other lover and proposes to him that they should play for her in a game of dominoes, the winner to keep the girl and to shoot the loser. Passereau loses, as he had planned to do, and, as his last request, begs his rival to go to the well in the garden and to look down into it. After this he dies happy for he knows that his enemy's victory is vain and that he will only find the corpse of his dead mistress in the well.

That is not however all that there is to this story. It contains more of Borel's dark humour than the other tales. There is a very Baudelairean scene where Passereau, in his first despair at discovering the treachery of his mistress, goes to the public executioner to ask him to guillotine him. 'Je désire que vous me guillotinassiez!' he says. It is a scene that would have appealed to Baudelaire in his youth. The discussion between Passereau and the executioner, when trying to persuade him, is highly comic. The latter protests that he has no sanction to perform such an act. Passereau however assures him that he does not expect an important public execution, but a simple little private one in a back garden, that would do. The executioner is a civil servant who cannot do anything that is not 'en règle'. The case must first go through the police and law courts, he says, before he can do anything. If all that is complied with, then he will be Passereau's most humble servant and make a clean and satisfactory job of it, he assures him.

We find in *Passereau l'Écolier*, in anticipation, the substance and atmosphere of the *Spleen* poems of Baudelaire, indeed it may well have been here that he found inspiration. Borel called these days, days of 'spleen' of 'splénalgie', days of 'néant'. 'Or donc les jours pluvieux, lourds et bas, les temps de bise, de brouillard, de bruine, il tombait dans le marasme, il soupirait vaguement, il s'ennuyait, il pleurait, dans une apathie désespérante; tout son refrain était: *la vie est bien amère et la tombe est sereine*, à bas la vie . . . *Les jours à néant* de Passereau n'étaient pas toujours l'effet de brume, de pluie et de temps noir; souvent, comme en ce cas, ils provenaient d'ennui, de contrariété et de chagrin.'[4]

The collection ends with *Testament de Champavert*, a tale full of bitterness and rancour against life, with no belief or hope in anything. 'Well! No! Idiots that you are! You are all going where everything goes, to nothingness! And it is, face to face with death, and my feet in the grave, cowards, that I say that to you! I don't want another life! I've had enough of life! It is nothingness that I long for!' Then Champavert blasphemes against God with the same violence as Baudelaire in the *Reniement de Saint Pierre*. 'And besides, you Christians, you hanged your God, and you were right, for if he had been God, he would have deserved hanging!'[5]

In this story, which is intentionally biographical, one sees the crack in Borel's personality which nothing will be able to mend. 'When a tree has been struck by lightning, no spring can ever again make it grow green.'[6] We do not however know what thunderbolt blighted him.

Champavert eventually makes a suicide pact with his mistress Flava because there is nothing left for him in life; he does not however formulate his grievances, but only raves against society in general, for it is society which has caused the death of his illegitimate son. His mistress bore it secretly, killed it at birth and buried it in the garden. 'Horrible world! A girl has to kill her son, or else she loses her honour. Flava, you are a girl of honour and you murdered yours!' Then to prove to her that there is no after life, to her who had expected some compensation in the hereafter, he digs up the corpse of their child and, holding it up before her, says, 'Flava, Flava, look at your son! Here! this is what eternity is, look!' Then he cries out against the world: 'Law! virtue! horror! Are you satisfied? Here take back your prey! Cruel world, that is what you wanted! Look! This is your work! Are you pleased with your victory? Are you pleased with your victories? Bastard! It was impudence on your part to have been born without royal consent, without banns! Barbarous law! Cruel prejudice! Infamous horror! Men, society! Here take back your prey! I give him back to you!'[7] And he flings the little skeleton away, so that it rolls down the slope and is broken to pieces on the stones of the road. Then he kills Flava with his dagger, goes down the hill and disappears into the fog. Next day a child's skeleton is crushed to dust beneath the wheels of a cart, the body of a woman is discovered near the stream with a dagger wound in her heart, and later a man covered in blood is found, lying in the road with a knife stuck in his breast.

Champavert's violence and pessimism are not explained. The improbability of the plot detracts from the impression of bitterness and *spleen* which would have been more effective without the *grand guignol* plot.

Champavert's revolt against the Romantic convention that nature is always beautiful, is similar to Baudelaire's and he too complains of the monotony, 'the eternal face of nature; always sun and rain; always spring and autumn, heat and cold; always and forever. Nothing more boring than something which never changes, than a fixed fashion, than a perpetual calendar. Every year the trees are green, and always green trees, always rain and sun, ever and always green trees. How boring that is! Why not more variety? Why should the leaves not assume, one after the other, all the coloursof the rainbow? Fontainebleau, how stupid all that greenery is!'[8]

Similar to Baudelaire's also is his hatred of Romantic love. 'Qu'ils viennent donc les imposteurs, que je les étrangle!' he cries. 'Les fourbes qui chantent l'amour, qui le *guirlandent* et le *mirlitonnent*, qui le font un enfant joufflu, joufflu de jouissances, qu'ils viennent donc, les imposteurs, que je les étrangle! Chanter l'amour ... pour moi, l'amour c'est de la haine, des gémissements, des cris, de la honte, du deuil, du fer, des larmes, du sang, des cadavres, des ossements, des remords, je n'en connaîs pas d'autre!'[9]

Champavert, in the midst of all the desolation around him, sees no issue except in suicide to escape the view of all the horror. It did not seem to him that there was anything that he personally could do. Life was a loathsome play, a loathsome farce which he was forced to watch, and which he refused to watch to the end. Barbey d'Aurevilly was to say, after reading *Les Fleurs du Mal* of Baudelaire, that their author, after composing such a book into which he had poured all his suffering and bitterness, had no other path left open to him but suicide or conversion. Champavert, in similar circumstances, chose suicide.

Champavert is the work in which Borel poured most of himself. Yet, with this bitterness and hatred of life, we find as well, compassion and sympathy for those who are obliged to endure the farce, especially for those who are simple and lowly. There was in him, in spite of his obsession with sadism—which was really an expression of deep hurt—a hatred of evil and a love of nobility and disinterestedness, a loathing for the vulgarity and materialism which he saw around him. These characteristics in Borel were later to endear him to Baudelaire who had similar revulsions.

Perhaps Borel really believed, after all, that it was only the surface that was rotten, and that in the depths there was purity; per-

haps that was why he chose a verse from a poem by his friend
Gérard de Nerval for the title page of *Champavert,* a poem which
expresses such hope.

> *Car la société n'est qu'un marais fétide*
> *Dont le fond, sans nul doute, est seul pur et limpide*
> *Mais où ce qui se voit de plus sale, de plus*
> *Vénéneux et puant, vient toujours par-dessus!*

Chapter 5

LA BOHÊME DU DOYENNE

<hr/>

The *Bouzingo* confederacy broke up not long after the publication of *Feu et Flamme* and *Champavert*. The group had been typical of the disturbed state of mind during the first years of the reign of Louis Philippe, when he was not yet accepted and there were constant revolts, but the courageous conduct of the King in July 1835 during the attempt on his life by Fieschi and during the slaughter which followed it, turned many people towards him and it could then be said that republicanism was dead. Henceforth the large bulk of the population settled down peacefully under his rule to make money and to build up the prosperity of the country. The *Bouzingos* were now beginning to be divided by quarrels and jealousy. Some were beginning to question the supremacy of Petrus Borel and to resent his ascendancy. It was also being whispered in some quarters that he did not fulfil his early promise, that he might be no more than an eccentric, that he might, in the words of Gautier, be only a damp squib which had misfired.[1] Gautier seemingly now felt that he no longer wished to worship at Borel's shrine but wanted one of his own. He was no longer the youth who, at the *Bataille d'Hernani*, had been carried away by the glamour of the man two years his senior. He was growing tired of the Borel fashion; he himself had no desire to be a lycanthrope. On the contrary he was a sociable *méridional* who liked to live at peace and in happiness with his friends; he liked good food and wine, and much preferred to get his teeth into rare beefsteaks than into red hot iron. Borel's long and sad face, his bitter view of life, began to get on his

BACCHANTES TAMING TIGERS
From the frescoes by Chasseriau on the
walls in Gautier's flat in Impasse du
Doyenné

nerves, and he considered that his arrogance was uncalled for. He began to see through his former ideal and to realise how much play-acting there was in Borel's pose of eccentricity and Byronic gloom. 'He was born to be an actor' he said of him, 'he should always have played the part of Anthony!'*

Others too, besides Gautier, were growing tired of the charnel house. When Gautier broke away from the circle of the Rue d'Enfer he bore away with him many of Borel's followers— Célestin Nanteuil, Gérard de Nerval, Auguste Maquet and others. Only Philothée O'Neddy remained faithful to Borel, but he had by then almost entirely abandoned literature and was working in his government office.

Gautier now made his own little circle in his new rooms in the Impasse du Doyenné, a little street near the Palais Royal which was later pulled down when the Place du Théâtre Français was built. Balzac has given a description of this old quarter in his novel *La Cousine Bette*, and Gérard de Nerval has described the house in his *Premier Château de Bohême*. Gautier had a small *garçonnière* for which he paid only about ten pounds a year. There he lived with Camille Rogier, Gérard de Nerval and Arsène Houssaye. The latter was a link between the bohemians and the Dandies for he was a close friend of Roger de Beauvoir and often brought him to the Impasse du Doyenné. This link with the Dandies somewhat changed the outlook of the young men so that they became less wild. They now called themselves *La Bohême du Doyenné* and Gautier, who had once studied painting, gathered round him a group of artists some of whom were later to become famous. There were Delacroix, Corot, Théodore Rousseau and Chasseriau, amongst those who are well known. There were also the former *Bouzingos* Célestin Nanteuil, Devéria and Boulanger.

Gautier, following the prevailing fashion of the thirties, gave a spectacular house-warming. He was determined however that his party was not going to be the wild carousing which had been a feature of Borel's house-warming. It was going to be a more artistic entertainment and alcoholic drink was not to be its chief attraction. This party, which was one of the most famous of the

* *Anthony* a play by Alexandre Dumas.

time, was held in November 1835. As Gautier possessed no pictures his friends decided that they would decorate his rooms for the occasion, especially the immense salon. Célestin Nanteuil drew a couple of druids over the frames of the doors. Théodore Rousseau painted two of his landscapes; Auguste de Châtillon produced a magnificent panel representing a monk in a scarlet habit reading a Bible which was supported on the naked body of a woman. Corot painted two landscapes of Provence of great originality it is said, and they must have been amongst his earliest works. Camille Rogier painted Gautier dressed as a Spaniard, and finally Chasseriau produced a group of Bacchantes holding a team of tigers on a leash like a pair of dogs. The sad thing is that most of the pictures are now known only through their description.[2] Gautier's landlord, who lived himself on the ground floor, finally, after two years of endurance, growing weary of the incessant noise above his head, gave them notice, and he covered over the paintings with a coat of white-wash as he considered that the nude or outlandish figures would hinder his letting the rooms to bourgeois tenants. Eventually, when the house was being pulled down, Gérard de Nerval tells us[3] that he was able to buy up from the house-breakers some of the panels—the two by Célestin Nanteuil, the Provence landscapes by Corot, the red monk by Châtillon, and the Bacchantes by Chasseriau.

Rumours of the house-warming had spread abroad and there were many gate-crashers, some even from the fashionable world, but the greatest number were poets, painters and members of the acting profession. As was usual in all parties at the time, fancy dress was compulsory, and it is said that some of the costumes were superb. It was then that Roger de Beauvoir appeared dressed as a nobleman from a picture by Veronese, and it suited his Italian beauty. It was composed of apple-green damask brocaded with silver, a doublet of orange silk and a velvet cap, while a heavy gold chain hung round his neck.[4]

Artistically the party was very brilliant, and many of the guests contributed to make the evening memorable. Mademoiselle Plessy from the Comédie Française, and Monsieur Lory from the Opera, produced a *ballet-pantomime* entitled *Le Diable Boiteux* which was

A BACCHANTE
From the frescoes by Chasseriau
in Gautier's flat in Impasse du
Doyenné

composed by Burat de Gurgy and which, a few months later at the Opera, was to make the fame of Fanny Elser. There was also a *parade*, *Le Courrier de Naples*, in which Edouard Ourliac delighted his audience by playing the part of harlequin. There was a further *parade* by Ourliac himself called *Le Temps de la Jeunesse ou la Jeunesse du Temps*, for which Gautier had written a prologue which he recited himself, hidden behind a curtain, while Burat de Gurgy, playing the part of a musician, accompanied the words from an improvised stage with appropriate dumb-show.

It can be judged by these dramatic interludes that Gautier's entertainment reached a far higher standard artistically than Borel's had done, when the deadly punch had been drunk out of skulls, when the *Galop Infernal* had been danced, ending in the street outside. Gautier's had less wildness and it needed more developed artistic sense to appreciate it.

A highly developed—often over-sensitive—artistic sense will be the chief quality of the literary fashion which was just about to begin, that of the Art for Art's Sake Movement. It was in violent contrast to the Satanism and lack of discipline of the *Bouzingos*. Gautier's party of November 1835 marks the end of Petrus Borel's supremacy and influence. It marks the end, for a time, of the charnel-house phase in French literature. Now for half a century it is the pseudo-classical influence, against which Baudelaire alone revolted, which will prevail. The new taste is seen in Gautier's *Mademoiselle de Maupin*, published in 1836, the provocative preface of which served as a manifesto for the new movement.

In the meantime, in 1835, Petrus Borel, left alone without followers and livelihood, felt bitterness growing in him, which he will pour out in his next book, *Madame Putiphar*. Yet, in spite of everything, his pride and arrogance did not abate. If all deserted him, he would still remain true, he alone, to the *Bouzingo* doctrine.

Chapter 6

MADAME PUTIPHAR

After the publication of *Champavert*, from which he had hoped so much but which was a financial failure, Borel's fortunes began to deteriorate very rapidly. He was as poor now as he had been when he had first joined the *Petit Cénacle*. He was even obliged, through lack of money, to do away with his beloved spaniel because he could no longer afford to feed it.[1]

He still kept up his connection with the literary world and contributed, whenever they would accept his work, to various women's papers—*Le Livre de Beauté* and *Le Journal des Demoiselles*—and to the literary periodical *L'Artiste*, a couple of critical articles and a short story, *Jerôme Chassebœuf*, which is sentimental and improbable, also below the achievement of *Champavert*. These contributions were few in number and not of a nature to earn him either fame or fortune. By degrees he fell deeper into poverty and despair. He had plans in his head for further works, plans which, unfortunately, he never fulfilled. He began a play, *Le Comte d'Alcaros*, which was never finished and he announced two novels, *Le Rossignol* and *Madame Putiphar*—the latter alone was eventually completed.

Finally, to escape from his poverty, to flee from a world he was gradually growing to hate—and this hatred was no longer a pose —he left Paris behind him and retired to the solitude of the country, to a little village in Champagne, Le Baizil, and there he lived alone in a wooden shack, originally intended to hold garden tools. He was no longer dressed in his smart black clothes, but in the uncouth rags of a tramp. There, with his own hands, he cultivated the little strip of ground which went with the hut, and grew the few vegetables which were now his only food in his near starvation diet.[2] The worst effect of hunger is not in the resulting physical pangs, but in the lowering of the spirits and in the black pessimism which it engenders. Solitude and hunger still further embittered him and turned him more violently against the world, and even against his former friends in Paris—against all except faithful Philothée O'Neddy whose depression and disillusionment in the civil service matched his own. The others, Gautier, Gérard de Nerval, Célestin Nanteuil and the rest, had now new interests and worshipped at other shrines. With O'Neddy alone did Borel keep up relations and it is he who undertook any literary business in Paris which Petrus Borel needed to be done.

The depression and weakness following hunger and illness made work slow for the poor lycanthrope. Fever sometimes kept him in bed for weeks on end without his being able to flog himself to work. He felt that he had lost not only belief in others but confidence in himself as well. The work which eventually emerged from his solitary retreat, *Madame Putiphar*, bears evidence of this lack of faith in the value of what he was writing. Little by little however the bitterness of his life was distilled in that book and the resulting liquor is harsh and fiery like wood alcohol, like the produce of an illicit still. Everything most horrible which could be devised by human imagination, every cruel trick of fate, every form of vengeance, are found between the covers of this terrible and gruesome book.

It was however proceeding at a snail's pace and he was not even deriving the sublime relief, the catharsis, of artistic composition. To O'Neddy, who wrote to him for news of the book, he answered, in 1836:[3] 'I have been working without respite— especially during the last fortnight—but, in spite of that, it does not progress very fast. How difficult it is to produce even an in- different book! Is it because the task undertaken is too difficult? Or that the labourer is too weak? I don't know, but I often feel myself giving way and breaking down under the weight of the burden. How often, during these last three days, have I not envied the fate of those who can produce books without this Hell, who each quarter can throw off a novel as a coachman flings off his boots. As for your humble servant, even working like a galley slave, he has at least another month of torture ahead of him. It is thus, seated by a fire of wood and straw in my hut, that your friend, with enormous clogs on his feet, with the rags of an old sail thrown over his shoulders, writes to you.

Written at Baizil, Lycanthropolis, Tuesday 29th, February 1836.'

Some time later he writes: 'I'm writing to you from my desert; I've sold my two volumes of *Madame Putiphar* for two hundred francs to Ollivier, and he is keeping back the last quarter of the money until the whole manuscript is finished. My poverty is extreme. I'm obliged to creep out of my cave in Bas-Baizil to glean my food in the fields.'

Ollivier would only pay, quarter by quarter, as the script was sent to him, and no entreaties from its author would soften his heart. Borel often regretted his previous and more generous publisher, Renduel, whose assistance he sought in his quarrel with Ollivier. To the latter he had written:[4] 'Monsieur, first may I take the liberty of bringing to your notice—to borrow an expression from you yourself—how *indelicate* it is for you to send an un-stamped letter to a man who works for you, and to whom you insist on refusing the fruits of his work; to a man, in short, who, thanks to your kind attentions, is in so dire a state of poverty that he had not even the ten sous to pay for your missive. Yes, Monsieur, I owe the postage on your letter to the postman who brought it. I said to the poor man: "Take it back for I've nothing to pay you with! I've nothing left at all!" But this good fellow, who —like the labourers here who lend me bread and potatoes—has not a shop-keeper's soul, gave it to me. What do you think of this action?

I don't understand at all on what calculations you base so regularly your refusal. But what I know well, and what you ought to have known even better, is that, at the time of the signing of the arrangement with Renduel, the second volume of *Madame Putiphar* had already reached the FOURTH sheet. Now the printers have at least enough for up to fifteen sheets. I've thus handed in recently the substance of ten sheets. For these ten sheets you have given me in all one hundred francs. I don't think that you've risked very much. It is not I, check it up, who am in your debt. I have in my possession the copy of the fifteenth and sixteenth sheets which I shall hand on to Monsieur Terzuolo one of these days, as soon as I think he deserves them. If the volume which I'm finishing is only to have twenty sheets, as you wish it you shop-keeper, but as I, novelist, do not wish it, you have then only six more sheets to get. If you add it up you'll see I'm right. A man who for a mere hundred francs, has handed in ten sheets of a text, is expected, for the same price, to give six more. That is too great a lack of confidence, believe me.

If the fifty francs, which you owe me, are not paid to me, if your conscience allows you to keep the wages of the workman, it is not, as it seems my friend Monsieur Dondey must have told you, *Madame Putiphar* who will suffer. No! Sir! it is I alone, unless—which God will certainly not permit—I succumb under the weight of need before I have been able to finish the work which He entrusted to me as a sacred trust. You think it a joke to make another man suffer the pangs of hunger, to make your workman suffer the pangs of hunger, whose delicacy you hold against him as a crime. A curious taste!

Your most obliged servant.'

Madame Putiphar was only finally completed in 1838.

While he was at Bas-Baizil Borel did however publish a book, a translation of *Robinson Crusoe*, printed at the press of his brother Francisque. It may have been his own wild and primitive life which prompted him, in a spirit of sympathy, to take an interest in the adventures of a man who had to provide for his daily life through his own efforts alone.

However, what Baudelaire was to call *le guignon* still pursued him. While he was working on his own translation, by a curious coincidence—these coincidences are not rare in literature—another translation was being prepared by Madame Tastu. Hearing of this just as his own translation was finished, Borel was inspired to write a preface which is a typical example of his pride

and arrogance. Having dismissed the achievement of his predecessors in translation with contumely, calling them 'a colourless
dilution devoid of eloquence' he goes on to call Madame Tastu's
effort androgynous, adding that 'la galanterie' prevents him from
giving an honest opinion. Finally he turns to his own translation
and says that, with all due modesty, he thinks that it is vastly
superior to any previous one. He then asks 'Will the public be
grateful to the author for the trouble he has taken? Will it dis-
criminate between work undertaken from choice and work done
rapidly for the sake of gain? Surely this must happen or otherwise
it would be too discouraging!'

Borel is here making a virtue of necessity, and drawing pride
from his lack of popular success, and the slowness with which he
always wrote. Yet he, no less than Madame Tastu, worked to earn
money and he needed it badly. She, a woman of spirit, did not sit
down quietly under his attack. On her side, she criticised his translation on the score of his having rendered what she called the naive
and simple speech and philosophy of *Robinson Crusoe* in pretentious
language, in the 'empty nonsense of a pseudo-poetic and romantic
prose'. With feminine intuition she here detects Borel's greatest
weakness, the affectation of his style and his tendency towards
pedantry. This fault is apparent largely in the reflective passages,
for the narrative and dialogue are successful and faithful to the
original. His pedantry is seen in his preface and in his footnotes,
and in his old-fashioned spelling. In the notes, lengthily and often
unnecessarily, he calls attention to the mistakes of his predecessors
and some of these certainly make comic reading.

Eventually Borel's translation outlived that of Madame Tastu
and of the others. Nearly half a century later when the publisher
Jouaust wanted to bring out a translation of *Robinson Crusoe* in his
Bibliothèque Artistique it was Borel's that he chose.

Borel's *Robinson Crusoe* was one of the first commercial books to
publish woodcuts as illustrations, and his old friends, the Devéria
brothers, Célestin Nanteuil, Boulanger, Napoléon Thom, and
others, were the illustrators. The volume is a fine example of
nineteenth-century printing and does credit to Francisque Borel.

A year later he had not yet finished *Madame Putiphar*, and, in a letter to O'Neddy who was his go-between with the printers he wrote: 'I'm sending you chapter XV of *Notre Dame Putiphar* to take, as you've done the previous ones, to the printers. I'd hoped to send it sooner and to send you more, but I've just spent a week in bed and that has impeded my progress a great deal. I also began working on chapter XVII without first finishing chapter XVI which will be needed first by the printers.'[5]

Finally he ground out the last lines of *Madame Putiphar*. Then he despatched the manuscript to O'Neddy and waited for the Censors to give permission to print. But they were very slow in granting it and to O'Neddy, who asked whether he had heard anything, he answered: 'No! their excellencies have sent nothing to Baizil up to the present, and I've not yet seen the faintest sign of a permission to print. I said to myself, these gentlemen, the High and Mighties, from the top of their virtuous perch, must have turned down my request, not wishing to connive at the publication of so monstrous a piece of immorality as *Madame Putiphar*. Judging from the label they must have augured so for the contents of the bottle.'[6]

Borel here presumes too much for his book—or is unfair to it, according to one's views. It is a novel in which every cruelty and horror are depicted, but it contains, no more than did *Champavert*, little immorality as such.

The book is dedicated to a mysterious A.L.P., but it is now known that these initials are those of Lucinda Paradol, called, in her day, the Queen of Tragedy, who was a leading actress at the Comédie Française. Unfortunately all those who have written about Borel at the time have been so discreet that we know nothing of their relations. What did the successful actress feel for the struggling poet whom most would regard as a failure? Perhaps they had been lovers in his days of glory when he was still full of promise and hope. Perhaps he had only worshipped at her shrine from afar, hoping one day to produce the masterpiece which he would lay at her feet, the great play which would bring fame to both of them. One of his last poems, published in *L'Artiste* six years afterwards, in May 1844, expresses the hope that he will write such a work, which he will bring to her and then, having acted in it, she will finally give him his reward. Perhaps he never did receive that reward since the play was never written.

Tout ce que vous voudrez pour vous donner la preuve
De l'amour fort et fier que je vous dois vouer;
Pas de noviciat, pas d'âpre et dure épreuve
Que mon cœur valeureux puisse désavouer.

Oui, je veux accomplir une œuvre grande et neuve!
Oui, pour vous mériter, je m'en vais dénouer
Dans mon âme tragique et que le fiel abreuve
Quelque admirable drame où vous voudrez jouer!

Shakespeare applaudira; mon bon maître Corneille
Me sourira du fond de son sacré tombeau!
Mais quand l'humble ouvrier aura fini sa veille,

Eteint sa forge en feu, quitté son escabeau,
Croisant ses bras lassés de son œuvre exemplaire,
Implacable, il viendra réclamer le salaire.'[7]

Madame Putiphar finally appeared in 1839 in two volumes, with a woodcut as frontispiece in each volume. A copy was inscribed to his old friend Philothée O'Neddy:

A Monsieur mon cher Frère
Théophile Dondey, offert du plus profond de mon cœur.
Petrus.

Jules Claretie, who brought out the second edition in 1877, says in his Preface that Borel found the subject for the novel in a book by Camille Desmoulins called *Révolution de Flandre et de Brabant*. In this work the author quotes a letter from a certain Macdonagh who complains that he was thrown into prison through the machinations of his colonel who wished to seduce his wife. This may well be so but this episode is only a fraction of Borel's complicated and diffuse novel. Arthur Symons, on the contrary, believes that Borel obtained his material from a book by Henri Masers de Latude entitled *Le Despotisme dévoilé ou Mémoires de*

Henri Masers de Latude détenu pendant trente cinq ans dans diverses prisons d'état, published in 1790.[8] Henri de Latude was thrown into prison at the age of twenty-three because he had earned Madame de Pompadour's displeasure, and he cites cases of other men imprisoned for the same reason. Borel's main plot is nearer to this than to Desmoulin's book. Also, in the second volume of *Madame Putiphar*, he mentions that a certain Henri Masers de Latude had been before Fitz-Whyte in the same dungeon, that his name had been carved into the wall. This means that he knew of de Latude and of his fate. There is no reason why he should not have occupied the prison in which Borel's character was later to be incarcerated, since he had been in so many of the prisons of France. There is also no reason why Borel, who was a voracious reader of historical material, should not have used both sources. In any case both of them together form only a small portion of the total novel which is largely of its author's own invention.

Madame Putiphar is exceedingly long and rambling, without any visible unity so that it is difficult to determine what really is the plot—if indeed there is any at all. It begins in Ireland, in the estates of a sadistic old Irish lord called Cockermouth who ill-treats his wife and daughter. On the estate lives a poor lad called Patrick Fitz-Whyte, a clever boy who is being educated with Deborah the daughter of the Lord. They naturally fall in love and meet secretly by night in the castle demesne. They are both young and innocent and they do nothing but talk of the former glories of Ireland and of their love. After many pages Deborah plans to elope with Patrick to France where he will enlist in the army. Her father discovers her plot and plans to shoot Patrick but, accidentally, wounds his daughter instead. Patrick flees abroad but tells Deborah how she will be able to find him when she reaches Paris; he will write his address in chalk on the walls of the Louvre. In Patrick's absence Lord Cockermouth gets him tried and condemned to death for the attempted murder of his daughter. She eventually manages to make her way to Paris and finds Patrick. They marry but the colonel of his regiment catches sight of Deborah, is struck by her beauty and determines that she shall be his. There follow many pages of his vain attempts at seducing her, of her defence of her virtue. Realising that he will not reach his ends the colonel determines to get rid of Fitz-Whyte.

In the meantime Patrick's closest friend, Fitz-Harris, has got himself into difficulties with Madame Putiphar—intended as a picture of Madame de Pompadour—because he has lampooned her in his writings, and she gets him sent to the Bastille. Fitz-Whyte obtains his pardon from the lady but, unfortunately, she falls in love with him at first sight when he comes to plead for his friend, and determines to seduce him. He nobly withstands her blandishments and finally says to her, quoting from Rousseau, 'The wife of a coalman is more worthy of praise than the mistress of a king.' Baudelaire was probably thinking of this passage, when he once retorted, while he was working on a paper in Dijon, when some people complained of his mulatto mistress, 'Sir, the mistress of a poet is better than the wife of a country attorney.'

Madame Putiphar apparently has an unlimited number of free 'lettres de cachet' for she manages to send both Fitz-Whyte and Fitz-Harris to the Bastille. Deborah, in the meantime, has been told that her husband has been killed. Then she is kidnapped one Sunday while she is hearing Mass, and taken to a certain establishment to be trained for Pharaon's bed—he is intended as a portrait of Louis XV. Next follows an absurd description of this superior brothel in which her training takes place, and of the behaviour of the Lesbian Madame in charge of it. The atmosphere is very similar to that of *La Religieuse* of Diderot. When Deborah is finally brought to the King she repulses him and, when he sees that nothing is to be gained from her, she too is sent to prison.

All the main characters are now in captivity. In prison Deborah gives birth to Patrick's son and christens him Vengeance. After many vicissitudes she manages to escape and she brings up her son in the ideal that he must one day avenge his father—hence his name.

The greater part of the novel henceforth deals with a description of the treatment meted out to Fitz-Harris and Fitz-Whyte in the state prisons of France. This permits Borel to give full rein to his obsession with horror and his talent for describing it. There is also compassion and tenderness, as in the account of the death of Fitz-Harris in the dungeon which he shares with Fitz-Whyte.

When Vengeance is sixteen his mother despatches him to fight with his father's colonel and to kill him. The colonel is now an old man, but it is the boy who is killed in the duel, and his slayer ties his corpse to his horse and sends it back to his mother.

After many years and many more chapters of horror we reach the moment of the storming of the Bastille in 1789 when only one prisoner is found, an old man who jabbers incomprehensibly in English and Irish. It is discovered that this is Fitz-Whyte, Deborah's husband. She is summoned to the prison to take him home, but she finds that he is mad and does not recognise her. She falls down dead through grief and shock.

Summarised briefly the plot has some coherence, but, as one reads, this is lost from sight in the six hundred odd pages full of digressions and irrelevancies. One cannot help wondering what it was that inspired Borel to embark on this theme. It may have been to give expression to his taste for horror, and he gives us in full measure, more than thirty years of torture and suffering in the state prisons of France in the eighteenth century. He did not realise that undiluted horror is not a suitable atmosphere for a novel, and that it soon ceases from having any effect at all. Horror, mystery and fantasy find their most perfect expression in the short story where the atmosphere can be swiftly conjured up and where the interest does not lie in full analysis of character, where facets of the personality and impressions are all that are needed to create the illusion. Then, when the tension has become well nigh unbearable, the blind can be swiftly pulled down and the light extinguished. That is why the tales of Poe and Hoffman will be remembered when the novels of horror will be forgotten, however great the talent that produced them.

Perhaps Borel's intention was to depict the evils of France under the old régime, evils due to one single woman. Yet Madame Putiphar appears only on two or three short occasions, dying in the early part of the novel. Perhaps we are supposed to believe that her disastrous stranglehold on France continued, even after her death, right up to the Revolution. This is manifestly absurd.

The book is written with all the bitterness of a pamphleteer of the revolutionary era, and the horrors of the prison occupy the largest part. But the days of the pamphleteers were over in the eighteen-thirties and the Bastille had been, for more than half a century, no more than a mark on the city pavement. By 1839 Frenchmen were beginning to consider the eighteenth century in a more kindly way, and they felt that the portraits of Louis XV and of Madame de Pompadour in *Madame Putiphar* were biased and unjust. They were not human beings but figures from melodrama and only in a revolutionary era could they have appealed to a public thirsty for the blood of tyrants. By 1839 Frenchmen were tired of hearing of the abuses of the old régime—they had known many of their own since then—the razing of the Bastille to the ground had not brought in the Millennium, and they were weary of hearing of the alleged debauchery and cruelty of the old nobility—the debauchery of their own bourgeoisie was sufficient for them.

The meaning of the book is contained in the first chapter, where Borel declares that he is going to prove that there are fated destinies, or as Baudelaire was later to say, that there are people who are pursued by 'le guignon', or a merciless fate. There are men who, in spite of the nobility of their natures, are the victims of misfortune, of events beyond their control, which they could not have foreseen and which no virtue on their part could have prevented. Borel says: 'If original sin is an injustice, then fated original destiny is a monstrosity.' He adds that he will not weary his head with reflecting on these odious considerations, nor try to explain what cannot be explained. He will only say that if there is a Providence, then it manifests itself in most strange ways, and woe betide the man who is thus branded. It would have been better if he had been stifled in his mother's womb.' That is the cry of Baudelaire in his poem *Bénédiction*.

Borel then says that he is going to relate the story of some horrifying destinies which he will not seek to explain, but will only suggest that his readers will be luckier than he if they can believe that a Providence has spun the thread of these lives, or if they can find a plan or a purpose in them.

This was his intention as he started to write but, by the end of the book, he had changed his mind and he says then that light had eventually come to him.[9] 'I do not know by what mysterious operation light came to me' and then, in many ecstatic pages he tries to explain the nature of this light. He believes now that there is after all a kindly destiny, a Providence that does look after Humanity; he believes now that the wicked do not triumph even on earth. Each receives eventually the wages he deserves and nothing remains unpunished. 'Yes! I believe in expiation! No! Fated original destiny is not a monstrosity, but a sublime law! God is the God of Vengeance!' He goes on to explain that God's vengeance is often invisible, often it takes a long time, but it is sure and inevitable in the end. God has eternity before him and has no need to hurry, but nothing escapes his sword.

This new belief is however no more consoling than the first, and no more just. Borel has, it is true, shown how cruelty and vice do not remain unpunished, but he has not explained the justice of the fate of the victims. It is true that the perpetrators of evil have ended violently, but so too have the innocent victims. Indeed everyone in the novel has reached a violent end. The innocent, Fitz-Harris, Fitz-Whyte, Deborah and their son Vengeance, says Borel, had to suffer for the evil of their parents and ancestors. He now admits that he had been wrong in the beginning when he had declared that Destiny had no plan. It has a plan, he says, and that plan is Vengeance.

In spite of his toil and trouble, one feels all through *Madame Putiphar*, effort rather than ease, and that he has flogged himself to his task, putting together material that never really fuses. It is a book that has been made rather than created. It has also been inflated with too much irrelevant matter, with too much pseudo erudition, with too many examples of his passion for pedantry and ostentatious learning. For instance he describes an excursion which Deborah made with the Governor of her prison into the country, and that is the pretext for a long historical disquisition on the former occupants of the island, for long botanical descriptions of the flora of the district. In another place, when Fitz-Harris' Colonel compares Deborah's hair to ebony, the young man answers:[10] 'Colonel, that is not a very accurate description. The varieties of ebony are very numerous!' Then he goes on to enumerate these and gives a list of five species, as well as black, white, grey, red and green ebony. 'Has the young lady red hair, green hair, black, grey or white hair?' He acts in a similar manner when her skin is compared to alabaster. Borel was always very proud of these *Quiz Programme* scraps of erudition which he had collected, and he spares his readers none of them. In the final chapter, where he begs for indulgence for any misprints that there may be in his books, he adds, with typical Borellian pride:[11] 'I hope that no one will attribute these misprints to carelessness or ignorance. I must say that those who might try to attack me on this score would make themselves perfectly ridiculous in the eyes of my friends, and in the eyes of all those who know me or my erudition, or my claims in this respect. As for me, who have their measure, they would only be pitiable in my eyes.' Yet, in spite of these assertions, Borel is not as accurate as he would like us to believe. He has a fine disregard for chronology and, for instance, describes Mirabeau as a prisoner in Vincennes prison, twelve years before he was incarcerated there, when he was only fifteen.

Madame Putiphar passed almost unnoticed and did not even enjoy the *succès de scandale* of *Champavert*. There was an article by Janin in the *Journal des Débats*,[12] an article of three pages violently attacking it as a very dangerous book. Not a single chapter found favour with him, and he compared Borel to the Marquis de Sade. It was the author himself who had asked Janin to review his book, thinking he would be favourable since he had written stories himself in the charnel-house vein in 1830—as for instance *L'Ane Mort*. But Janin had changed very much during the nine years since then and he now denied the style of his youth, thinking Sade the symbol of all that was evil. When Borel asked him to review his book he answered that he could only compare it to Sade. This did not however displease Borel who still admired the Marquis who figures in person in the novel as 'one of the greatest glories of France . . . Famous amongst the most famous'.

In his article Janin asks: 'What is a critic to do when faced with such a deplorable and dangerous work? Can he, with a clear conscience, allow such a book to pass unnoticed, one whose

premises are obscene and whose conclusion is bloody? Would he
be doing his duty, in face of such abuse of the mind, if he contented himself with deploring to himself in secret what he ought
to criticise openly?'

Janin is unduly hard on *Madame Putiphar* and finds no qualities
to admire in it. Yet there is in it good writing and many passages
of tragic poetic beauty. There is for instance the gruesome ride of
the dead body of Vengeance, lashed to his horse, through the
darkness, sent back to his mother by the man who slew him. There
is in this description a nobility which possesses epic grandeur.
Moving also is the account of the death of Fitz-Harris in his
dungeon. Baudelaire, a greater critic than Janin, was less severe
and, writing twenty years later, found much to like and to
admire, and evidence of a distinguished talent.

The most interesting part for readers today, now that the taste
for horror has vanished, is the Prologue in verse addressed to
A.L.P. One wonders why this poem was placed here for it has no
connection with the novel, and little too with the woman to whom
it is addressed. It was written for the greater part in the bitter and
agonising solitude of Baizil,[13] and it shows a marked advance on
the poems in *Rhapsodies*, in powers of expression, in depth and
maturity. Its symbolism has some of the quality which we shall
later find in Baudelaire, particularly the contrast between *Spleen*
and *Idéal*. The chief fault in Borel's poem is its excessive length
and some redundant passages which could have been omitted
with gain in effectiveness and concision.

> *Une douleur renaît pour une évanouie;*
> *Quand un chagrin s'éteint c'est qu'un autre est éclos;*
> *La vie est une ronce aux pleurs épanouies.*

The three knights appear, who symbolise the World, Solitude
and Death, and fight for possession of the poet's soul.

> *Dans ma poitrine sombre, ainsi qu'en un champ clos,*
> *Trois braves cavaliers se heurtent sans relâche,*
> *Et ces trois cavaliers, à mon être incarnés,*
> *Se disputent mon être, et sous leurs coups de hache*
> *Ma nature gémit; mais, sur ces acharnés,*

Mes plaintes ont l'effet des trompes, des timbales,
Qui soûlent de leurs sons le plus morne soldat,
Et le jettent joyeux sous la grêle des balles,
Lui versant dans le cœur la rage du combat.

The first knight is young and fresh, wearing elegantly his
corselet of steel which glistens through a net-work of green. His
eyes shine with happiness and his helmet is decorated with a tuft of
feathers. His arab horse waves its head with its long plumes and
the knight rides alone, his golden spurs shining in the sun, and he
waves his dagger like a toreador.

The second knight comes riding astride his mule, and on its
skinny back, where the ribs stand out like barrel hoops, a faded
cloth is thrown. He is a figure of fun, a carnival scarecrow. He is
a penitent monk who, to buy his seat in Heaven, withdraws from
the temptations of the world. He is stained with blood and em-
braces a crucifix.

The third knight is like the Captain from *Don Juan*, a sinister
figure, the skeleton at the feast.

Il porte à sa main gauche une faulx dont l'acier
Pleure à grands flots le sang, puis une chausse-trappe
En croupe où se faisande un pendu grimacier,
Laid gibier de gibet! Enfin pour cimeterre
Se balance à son flanc un énorme hameçon
Embrochant des filets pleins de larves de terre,
Et de vers de charogne à piper le poisson.

The first of these knights is the World who, to attract the poet,
crowns him with flowers and, like Sir Walter Raleigh before his
Queen, flings down his cloak in the muddiest part of the road for
him to step on. He begs him to surrender himself to him without
remorse. He opens wide for him the big folding doors to the
dance-hall of life and shows him the world of wine, women and
love, the world with its thousand loves, its whores, its balls and
its banquets. This is the world with all its vanity.

C'est le monde! Il me dit:—viens avec moi, jeune homme,
Prends confiance en moi, j'emplirai tes désirs;

Oui quelque grands qu'ils soient je t'en paierai la somme!
De la gloire, en veux-tu? . . . J'en donne! . . . Des plaisirs? . . .
J'en tue—et t'en tuerai! . . . Ces femmes admirables
Dont l'aspect seul rend fou, tu les posséderas,
Et sur leurs corps lascifs, tes passions durables
Comme sur un caillou tu les aiguiseras!'

The second knight is Solitude, he offers the desert where the
soul can feel raptures in its constant flood of spiritual light.

C'est le cloître! Il me dit:—Monte chez moi, jeune homme,
Prends confiance en moi, quitte un monde menteur
Où tout s'évanouit, ainsi qu'après un somme
Des songes enivrants; va, le seul rédempteur
Des misères d'en bas, va, c'est le monastère,
Sa contemplation et son austerité!
Tout n'est qu'infection et vice sur la terre:
La gloire est chose vaine, et la postérité
Une orgueilleuse erreur, une absurde folie!'

The last knight is Death: Then follows a true Baudelairean
description.

Niveleur éternel; implacable faucheur,
C'est la Mort, le Néant! . . . D'une voix souterraine
Il m'appelle sans cesse:—Enfant, descends chez moi,
Enfant, plonge en mon sein, car la douleur est reine
De la terre maudite, et l'opprobe en est roi!'

Death then tells him to come and to enjoy rare pleasures, to
enjoy them soon for time does not wait, and the eternal harvester
will come.

Viens plus tôt que plus tard, sans oubli je vendange
Un par un les raisins du cep Humanité.

And again he says:

Il n'est de bonheur, de repos qu'en la fosse:
Sur la terre on est mal, sous la terre on est bien;
Là, nul plaisir rongeur; là, nulle amitié;

Là, point d'ambition, point d'espoir déçu . . . Rien!
Là, rien, rien, le néant! . . . Une absence, une foudre
Morte, une mer sans fond, un vide sans écho . . . —

And the poems ends:

Ainsi, depuis longtemps, s'entrechoque et se taille
Cet infernal trio,—ces trois fiers spadassins:
Ils ont pris—les méchants pour leur champ de bataille,
Mon pauvre cœur, meurtri sous leurs coups assassins,
Mon pauvre cœur navré, qui s'affaisse et se broie,
Douteur, religieux, fou, mondain, mécréant!
Quand finira la lutte, et qui m'aura pour proie,—
Dieu le sait!—du Désert, du Monde ou du Néant?

Baudelaire greatly admired this poem and was influenced by it. It shows more mastery of expression and variety of image than any of Borel's previous poems, a surer and more moving symbolism.

Chapter 7

SATAN

After publishing *Madame Putiphar* in 1839 Borel decided to return to Paris and to make renewed efforts to earn his living through free-lance journalism. He also had further plans for original works. In 1838, on the cover of one of Gautier's books, he advertised an essay called *Aimez-vous la Cornemuse?* as appearing shortly, and on the back of *Madame Putiphar* as well as in the last chapter, he announced a novel in two volumes called *Tabarin* as already in the press, and another *Jeanniquette*, also in two volumes, as forthcoming. Only the latter was ever published and then not as a novel but as a short story which appeared in July 1839 in *La Presse*. It is the highly moral and edifying tale of a nobleman who loved a fisher-girl who however refused him because she did not think that such a marriage would turn out happily. Eventually he married a girl of his own class and Jeanniquette a man of hers. Later he tries to seduce her but she repulses him and he gives up all hope of winning her. Then her husband is kidnapped by corsairs and she, in order to provide for her starving children, goes to the castle to offer herself to the lord in return for payment. Touched by this act of self-sacrifice, he does not take her but looks after her children and eventually secures the release of her husband. The tale then ends happily and virtuously. Poor as it is as a short story it would have been poorer still if it had been inflated to form a two volume novel.

Better artistically are the ironically humorous sketches which he published in *Les Français peints par eux-mêmes*—*Le Gniaffe* and

Le Croquemort. They are good examples of his bitter irony, his 'humour noire', and his talent for the burlesque. It is a pity that he did not write more frequently in this vein. That he should have chosen, in his sketches of Frenchmen, to write on the undertaker is very characteristic, and his picture is painted with humorous seriousness. He describes the undertaker as interested in people only according to the amount of wood that was needed for their coffins. Ophelia for him meant only five foot by fifteen inches. When someone says to him 'so Monsieur is an undertaker' he answers 'Moi croque-mort? Non Monsieur, je ne suis pas croque-mort! Depuis l'An XII, Monsieur, il n'y a plus de ces hommes la! Je suis, Monsieur, Porteur Funèbre de Défunts à l'Entreprise Générale!'[1]

The undertaker says that he had disliked the time of the cholera, it was a deplorable time, when there was too much work to do it properly, and people were buried hastily without proper formalities. The 'Compagnie des Sépultures' had not sufficient black hanging, nor hearses, and the coffins had to be piled up anyhow. But at rich funerals, of 'un mort de première classe' or even of 'de bonne qualité' the master of ceremonies wore knee breeches and then his calves were of vital importance. A master of ceremonies of good quality cost ten francs, but if he had poor calves then he only got eight francs, while one with bandy legs might get as little as seven francs. The whole sketch is written in Borel's most brilliant style.

The literary world had changed very much during the years while Borel had been away from Paris. People had settled down peacefully under Louis Philippe and the day of revolt in politics and literature were over. Classical harmony and perfection of style were now fashionable. The descriptions we now have of Petrus Borel are very different from those of ten years before, when he was the glorious *Bouzingo*. Albert de la Fizelière, who was the Editor of *L'Artiste* when he returned to Paris, describes him as arriving one day at the offices of the paper looking for work and bringing with him a story to offer for publication. He expresses his surprise when he saw Borel, it was not the man he had expected. He saw a sad and gloomy individual, looking far older than his thirty-three years. He was already beginning to grow bald, his eyes were deep-sunk in his head, and he had a desperate and tragic expression; his back was bowed and he looked apologetic and somewhat ashamed of himself. This was a very different man from the magnificent figure who had fought at the *Bataille d'Hernani*. 'In his eyes', says Claretie 'on devinait bien des naufrages!'[2]

All his former companions had reached some measure of success and security. Petrus Borel alone was like a sailor stranded on some desert island from which all his comrades had sailed away. The short story which he brought to offer to *L'Artiste* was *Miss Hazel*, a tale which might have been written by a maiden-aunt for a girls' magazine. It was published by the paper in 1842.[3]

At this time he was also writing a considerable number of short, and probably ill-paid, articles for various papers: for *Le Commerce*, *Le Journal des Chasseurs*, *La Sylphide* and *La Revue de Paris*. Only two stories that he wrote at this time are worthy of notice; these are *Le Trésor de la Caverne d'Arcueil* which appeared in *La Revue de Paris* in April 1843 and *Gottfried Wolfgang* which came out in *La Sylphide* in the same year. The latter is probably Borel's best short story and it is a tale that Edgar Allen Poe might have written. It tells of the life of a German student in Paris during the Revolution. He specialises in occult philosophy, and, after much practice, has managed to create round himself a mysterious atmosphere in which strange things happen to him with the vividness of real life. For many years he has been haunted by the memory of a woman whom he had met in this dream existence, and whom he continued to love passionately although he had never seen her in real life. One night, during the Terror, as he wanders through the silent and deserted town, he suddenly sees the guillotine. The moon is shining on it and he sees, seated on its steps, a young woman dressed in black, with her hair hanging down her back. He immediately recognises her as the woman whom he had only met in his dreams. He goes up to her and speaks to her. She tells him that she has no relatives or friends in Paris, and that her last refuge has gone. He offers her the shelter of his room for the night and she accepts with alacrity. They walk along together through the horror of the empty streets, and he is more struck than ever by her beauty, by her long black hair, her white skin and her large sad eyes. Around her neck she wears a black velvet ribbon with a diamond clasp. As they walk he tells her of his love for her all these years and she admits to feeling a sudden attraction for him. When they reach his room she refuses his offer of his bed and sleeps in his arm-chair without undressing. Early next morning he goes out to find suitable lodgings for her and, on returning to his room, sees her lying in the chair, crumpled up with her head hanging down. He touches her hand and finds that it is cold. He looks into her white face and realises that she is dead. He weeps with anguish and the neighbours rush in to see what has happened. A policeman comes in with the others and, after he has looked at the girl, he steps back with amazement. 'How did this woman get here?' he asks; 'she died yesterday on the guillotine!'

Then Gottfried goes up to her and unfastens the diamond clasp at her throat; the velvet ribbon falls off and he sees, all round her neck, the mark of the knife still red with blood.

Dumas later stole this story and published it under the title *La Femme au Collier de Velours*. The theft was not recognised as few people had read it when it first came out in *La Sylphide*, and when it was republished under a false name Borel was in Algeria and had given up writing.

In 1844 Borel was once more the editor of a paper and it was very characteristically called *Satan*. It was not he however who gave it its name for it was so called when he took it over from his brother and he did not found it himself as stated by both his biographers. Indeed most of the facts given by Claretie and Aristide Marie concerning his connection with *Satan* are incorrect.

A paper called *Les Coulisses* was founded in December 1840. It was printed by Francisque Borel, and André Borel, another brother, used to contribute to it. Two years later, in February 1843, the paper announced that it was henceforth to be known by the name of *Satan*, and that Francisque Borel was to be its editor. It had on its title page a fine engraving of Satan looking out over the kingdom of the world, while he says 'If I were the King of evil, the monarch of corruption, I could say with pride "My good town of Paris!" ' The Satan of this paper is not the spirit of evil, but of truth, and his policy is to tell the truth to mankind without any fear of consequences. It is chiefly as the speaker of truth that Satan is feared, not as a corruptor, and he is going to hold the mirror up to mankind so that all men can see themselves in their hideous reality. He is going to write the memoirs of the human race, and the paper will be satiric. This Satanic connection was heralded even in the old *Coulisses*, for in the October number there is a cartoon which depicts a devil drawing back a curtain to reveal what is hidden behind it, and on his quiver full of arrows is written the word 'Satire'.

Satan appeared for the first time in February 1843 but it was not long before it got into trouble. In June of that year the editor was condemned to a month's imprisonment and to a fine of two hundred francs, for having published articles attacking the Chamber of Deputies and the Upper House. Francisque Borel was convicted of having published in *Satan*, in March, April and May, editorials in which he had discussed the actions of Ministers, Deputies and Lords, especially in a series of articles called *Journal des Victimes*. There was always a section devoted to gossip and malice. To give a couple of examples: One number said: 'The vast majority of statesmen are like the pavements of the Capital, that is to say in a state of complete collapse.' And another time: 'The waters of the Seine are muddy and filthy; that is because that river flows through Paris, the seat of the Government.'

Again in November the editor was taken to the Courts and this time was condemned to five months' imprisonment and a fine of five hundred francs for libel.

It was soon afterwards that Petrus Borel was made editor, in the absence of his brother, and he had charge of the paper from February 1844 until September of that year. No change of tone is discernible during his editorship. He wrote a great many of the articles—on art and literature, and book reviews. They are vividly written and in an individual style, and show that he could have become a very distinguished critic. He also published three poems

in *Satan*, which have never been republished. They do not however add anything to his reputation as a poet.

Satan however did not prosper and it was obliged to resign its
independence in September 1844. It then joined forces with another paper called *Le Corsaire* which had been going strong since
1822. The paper then called itself *Le Corsaire-Satan* and lasted
in that guise until 1847; then the *Corsaire* completely swallowed
up *Satan* and dropped the name which no longer had any meaning, and reverted to its former name of *Le Corsaire*. It was in *Le
Corsaire-Satan* that Baudelaire published some of his first com-
positions.

Borel next edited an illustrated paper. With a man called
Déchères he founded *La Revue Pittoresque*, and he intended to
obtain contributions from the best artists of the day, but the only
ones known to us today are Célestin Nanteuil, Gavarni and Tony
Johannot. He republished his *Miss Hazel* in the paper and most of
the contributions were reprints from the early works of Gautier,
Gérard de Nerval and Sainte-Beuve.

At this time Gérard de Nerval and Borel renewed their early
friendship and planned to set up a publishing house, something
similar to what Poulet Malassis was to achieve some years later,
that is they intended to publish elegant and well-printed works of
literary value, at a moderate price. They started with *Le Diable
Amoureux* of Cazotte with drawings by Edouard de Beau-
mont. They had further ambitions of bringing out a new translation of the Bible, and a collection called *L'Ane d'Or* which was
to print works by the modern followers of Lucian, Apuleius,
Quevedo, Boccaccio and Saint Evremond.

Nothing that they published brought in much money. Indeed
nothing sound could be expected from the collaboration of two
such madmen as Gérard de Nerval and Petrus Borel. *Satan* failed,
as did the *Revue Pittoresque* and *L'Ane d'Or*. Everything seemed
to fail Borel at once. He had been appointed manager of the
Société Générale de la Presse, founded by Dutacy, but the society
went bankrupt and he was never paid his salary.

The friend of his youth, Arsène Houssaye, became editor of
L'Artiste in 1844, and Borel hoped much from this. Houssaye, in

memory of their early friendship, gave him work regularly on the paper. Borel did not however publish in it the contributions one would have expected from him. No short stories and only five poems—three sonnets and two longer poems—which, though of a higher standard than those in *Satan*, do not add anything further to what we know of him as a poet.[4] His contributions largely consisted of articles in which he gave expression to his growing passion for scraps of erudition and rare knowledge.

It is sad that this interest should not have been more profitably exploited. He would have made a good academic teacher. He could then have cultivated his eccentricity to his heart's content, could have been as discursive as he liked with his pupils who would have been obliged to listen—in any case the young have a liking for oddments and scraps of knowledge; they would have been impressed by his erudition and moreover, even if the scraps of knowledge were useless, they would not have been any more so than many of the facts put together as academic research.

In *L'Artiste* Borel contributed such articles as *De la Chaussure chez les Anciens et les Modernes*, *De la Pantoufle*, *Philologie Humoristique*, *Pierre Beyle*, *Rêveries Ethnologiques*, and so forth. The last of his contributions was a pastiche of Montaigne, cleverly written and showing appreciation of his mind and style. This is *Du Jugement Publicque*.

Amongst the writers who gathered in the offices of *L'Artiste* Borel seemed of another age and world, of another generation, and yet he was the same age as Gérard de Nerval and Gautier. Champfleury describes him as a shabby middle-aged man—and yet he was only thirty-five—standing by the mantelpiece in the editor's office, and talking solemnly and grandiloquently in archaic language.[5] He still thought of himself as a leader, still tried to assert his ascendancy over others, especially over those whom he had known when he was young, and they now resented it. Houssaye describes him condescendingly in his *Confessions* as a 'decent chap', but complained that he would persist in thinking himself a leader. 'He preached too much, just as if he were a master.'

Only Baudelaire, himself at that time an artist struggling

against lack of means and comprehension, only Baudelaire, with his sympathy and understanding for failures, recognised something noble and fine in this tragic wreck, in the dark sad figure who came and went silently in the offices of *L'Artiste*; Baudelaire found him someone after his own heart; he admired his refusal to compromise, his inability to sell his soul for gain, his refusal to give in in spite of failure and suffering. Baudelaire already knew Borel's work and in his own early writings modelled himself on him. Life however eventually broke Borel as it was never to break Baudelaire, and he finally gave up the struggle and accepted servitude.

Eventually, for some reason never explained, Borel turned his eyes towards Algeria as if hope of salvation lay there. In this new colony, for which so many government projects were being made for development and colonisation, he thought some place might be found for him. He wrote an article called *Alger son Avenir Littéraire*, and published it in *L'Artiste* in November 1845.

This article gave his friends the idea of how they might help him, for most were very anxious on his behalf, and his poverty and misery were a constant reproach to them. One day Gautier met him as he was dragging himself wearily along the boulevard, looking as if he had not eaten anything for some days. 'I think I've found a job for you' said Gautier to him. 'What job?' asked Borel, wearily for he had suffered many disappointments. 'You've always said that you liked a wild life' answered Gautier, 'would you be willing to leave the country? Would you be willing to take a post in Algeria?' Borel, at this time, would have accepted a job even in Hell, for that would not have been a worse life than the one he was enduring.

Next Gautier spoke on his behalf to Emile de Girardin who told him of the chance of the appointment in Algeria for Borel as Inspector of Colonisation, and suggested that he should apply for it.

'Monsieur le Ministre' wrote Borel in his letter of application,[6] 'For a long time now my inclinations and interests have made me conceive of a great longing to go to Algeria, where my knowledge and aptitude ought, it seems to me, to find some outlet. I am informed that there are, at the present moment, several posts of Inspector of Colonisation vacant. I am confident that I have the necessary qualifications to fill one of these posts in a satisfactory manner, and I therefore request your Excellency to grant it to me.

I was brought up in the country in the district of Lyons and in the Alps, and most of my life I have lived there. I have specialised in rural economy—theoretical and practical—and I have done agriculture and manual work, also supervised farming. I have experience of cattle-breeding and I farmed myself a small property in the neighbourhood of Paris, the Commune of Baizil.[7] I would also like to add that I am an architect, that I have some skill and experience in draughtsmanship and practice. I was a student at the Ecole des Beaux Arts for several years. I have been employed as draughtsman and supervisor by several architects in Paris and in the provinces, I have helped in the construction of sixty buildings of different kinds and have myself built several houses in Paris which I could show if necessary.

I should also like to state that having cherished the hope for a long time of going to Algeria, I have begun to learn Arabic under the instruction of Doctor Perron, medical adviser to Méhémet-Aly, who is in Cairo, and that I intend to devote myself to the study of the language if, as I sincerely hope, your Excellency will deign to view favourably my application.

I beg most respectfully, Monsieur le Ministre, that you forgive my having expatiated at some length on those of my qualifications which might recommend me in your eyes, but your Excellency will see in this enumeration no more than the desire to obtain the position for which I feel that I have the taste, the qualifications and the conviction that I would carry out all my duties.

I add a few extra details which I think your Excellency might wish to have for the full appreciation of my application.

The absence from Paris of a large number of deputies and people in high places who pay me the compliment of being interested in me, does not permit me to enclose, with this application, all the references which would have supported it. Your Excellency, taking these circumstances into account, and also the urgency of the matter, will, I am sure, overlook all that may be missing, and will examine sympathetically my qualifications. It is your kindness that I rely on most, and this is my greatest hope.

If it is possible for you to grant me this appointment for which I most earnestly long, your Excellency will have the greatest and most beneficial influence on my future and will fill my heart with deep and lasting gratitude.

I have the honour to remain, Monsieur le Ministre, with the greatest respect, your humble and most obedient servant, Petrus Borel.'

This letter is typical of the pompous long-windedness of Borel's official correspondence. It will be seen that he lays no stress on his literary achievements—indeed does not mention them at all—thinking that they would be no recommendation.

Ten days after he wrote this letter Borel received notice that he had been appointed Inspector of Colonisation and that he was to sail from Marseilles on nineteenth January 1846 for Algeria, and that all his travelling expenses would be paid.

In the literary world in Paris this last eccentric exploit of the lycanthrope excited amusement as soon as the news spread of his appointment, on its appearance in the papers, and there was much ironic merriment at this new ending for Champavert, not a physical suicide, but a literary one.

The editor of Le National, an ambitious man in opposition to Louis Philippe, used Borel's appointment as a pretext to attack the government. 'They say' he wrote[8] 'that a man of letters who is not wholly unknown, had a sudden inspiration a few days ago, after he had lunched well, to go to the Ministry to ask for a concession of land in Algeria, and an advance of capital to start with. But, as he admitted to the clerk whom he interviewed, that he had no other aim but a pleasure trip, the clerk advised him to ask for a job instead, and offered him that of Inspector of Colonisation. The offer was gladly accepted, the application was despatched to the Minister, and two days ago he obtained the contract of Inspector of Colonisation. It is evident that the interests of Algeria are in as good hands as those of the metropolitan area.'

Borel was incensed when he read this article and complained to the editor, demanding an apology, but Marrast, the editor, only laughed and the *National* printed a further, and more insulting, article than the first one.

'We had borrowed' it said, 'from *L'Esprit Public* an article describing the appointment of a man of letters who is being sent to Africa as Inspector of Colonisation. This article was not flattering towards this writer and the paper apologised this morning. We have no opinion to express concerning the new Inspector, and we are unable to assess his qualifications or his special training, since we do not know him. But what we do know is that the Ministry of War is forever creating new posts which are completely redundant. And, as if it were not sufficient already with the extravagant wastes existing in Algeria, it adds to it by leaving in idleness a host of civil employeees of all sorts and sending fresh ones from here whose goodwill is no doubt excellent and who, while waiting for the opportunity of showing it in practice, have no other function than to receive the money of their salaries. The appointments they are given are very useful—that is for them —but assuredly the colony gains nothing from it, and the national budget loses by it. In big and in small matters the system seems to be always the same, that is to satisfy personal interests and to pay no heed to general utility and justice.'[9]

This time Borel sent his seconds to Marrast to challenge him to a duel, but he refused to see them. Then Borel thought of an action worthy of Champavert. He enlisted two of the heftiest porters from the central market, two *forts des Halles*, and sent them to Marrast. 'I'll send no more gentlemen seconds' he said. But the appearance of these two giants only made the editor burst into loud laughter, and he sent them away. Before Borel could again retaliate, his embarkation order arrived, and he was obliged to leave Paris. This was his last action on French soil and he was never again to return to his native land, nor ever to see again his relations and friends.

He arrived in Algeria on 25th January 1846.

Part Four

THE CIVIL SERVANT

Chapter 1

ALGERIA

When Petrus Borel arrived in Algeria in January 1846 the country was enjoying a more peaceful state than at any other moment under French rule. It had unfortunately happened that soon after its conquest in 1830 Charles X had been deposed, and during the first years of the reign of Louis Philippe there had been much social unrest in France the result of which was that all affairs not immediately connected with the home country were neglected. The Algerian expedition had not been popular with the new government, and for six years, until the social state had become stabilised once more, there had been no clear policy with regard to Algeria, for the government had been totally uninterested in the fate of the unfortunate men who had settled there. But in 1836, when the danger of revolution at home seemed past, a definite effort was made to exploit the new colony profitably. By a decree passed that year each settler was to receive, on provisional terms, the grant of a concession of land which would become his property in perpetuity as soon as he had fulfilled certain specified conditions which had been laid down for him. He had to possess a capital of fifteen hundred francs—about sixty pounds in the currency of the day—before he could apply for a concession, then he was granted a free passage to Algeria; on his arrival twelve hectares of land were allotted to him which he had to cultivate, and on which he was obliged eventually to build a permanent house. He was provided with temporary shelter and given building materials, agricultural implements, seed and beasts of burden, and, in some cases he was even granted a loan to tide him over the first months of residence. While he was engaged in creating a farm the army was occupied in building roads and employed gangs of convicts to clear away the bush and the scrub. This was later known as the heroic period in Algerian colonisation, but it failed unfortunately since all the colonists were eventually massacred by the natives.

Then, in 1840, General Bugeaud was sent to Algeria as governor and it was he who consolidated the French North African Possessions. On his arrival he discovered that the greatest obstacle to peace was the Arab Emir, Abd-El-Kader, who was trying to build up a large empire on his own and to evict the French settlers. To achieve this he had enlisted on his side the Moroccans, but they were defeated by Bugeaud at the Battle of Isly—it was after this that the General was created Duc d'Isly by Louis Philippe—and this put a permanent end to the ambitions and power of the Emir, for he was obliged to surrender to the French and was then interned for many years in France.

The way was now open for Bugeaud to carry out his projected reforms. His motto was *Ense et Aratro*—that is to say 'by the sword and by the plough' and he began to implement his own plans of colonisation. His intention was that the settlers should all be members of the armed forces or retired soldiers, so that they should be able to defend themselves against attack by the natives, as well as colonise the country. His main difficulty in carrying out his plan of colonisation was that the soldiers, as soon as their time in the army was over, used to abandon their concessions and return home to France. To put an end to this sorry state of affairs Bugeaud conceived the idea of importing wives from France for his soldiers and of creating a colony for retired soldiers at Fouka. He thought that if they were firmly established in the country with their wives and children they would no longer wish to leave on retirement. He then requested the Mayor of Toulon to collect a number of healthy young women who would be willing to marry soldiers when they retired, and to settle permanently in Algeria. The Mayor chose twenty amongst the deserving young women of Toulon and then Bugeaud despatched twenty soldiers

from Algeria to be paired off with the girls. The forty young
people were introduced, then collected in a room together, and
allowed to settle amongst themselves who was to pair off with
whom. Finally everything was satisfactorily concluded and the
pairs were taken to the Town Hall where they were united by the
Mayor. After that five hundred francs were given to each man and
two hundred to each girl, and they were sent to Algeria. The
marriages were said to have turned out very well in most of the
cases.

There was at first in Algeria great hostility towards the settlement at Fouka founded by Bugeaud, and he planned to create
sixteen similar centres so that they could support one another. In
1841 he devised a system of concessions, very like those of his
predecessors in 1836, the difference being that his settlers were
not civilians but soldiers or retired soldiers. He also brought in
new regulations to bind the settlers to their lands, since the first
concessions had led to many abuses and to much disastrous
speculation, because they had often been taken up by men who
had no intention of remaining permanently in Algeria. New
clauses were introduced to obviate this danger. The main regulations stipulated as follows: That the settlers were bound to build
houses in keeping with the size of their concessions; that they
were obliged to plant a specified number of trees per acre; to clear
their land of scrub and to put it under cultivation; to surround
their properties with a ditch, wall or hedge, or some kind of
permanent boundary.

All the clauses were made law on 4th May 1841; they reappeared
unaltered in the decrees of 21st July 1845, in those of July 1847,
and they lasted until the fall of Louis Philippe. To ensure that all
the regulations were observed in the far-flung domains of the
various provinces of Algeria, to keep an eye on the settlers and to
see that they did not allow their land to decay, a certain number
of inspectors were appointed by the Government and they were
called Inspectors of Colonisation. It was to one of these posts that
Borel was appointed in January 1846.

Bugeaud's plan of colonisation was the first to succeed in
Algeria since its conquest. It was he who changed the former

name of French Possessions of North Africa to that of Algeria. He divided the country into three provinces, and in each province he established by law which was to be civil territory, that is, not under the jurisdiction of the army, which to be mixed—that is, governed by the civil and military authorities—and finally which to be Arab territory. In Civil territory Europeans were allowed to settle as they pleased and to buy land there and build houses on it —Bugeaud's settlements were intended to be of this kind. The mixed territories, which usually lay in the suburbs of the town or in the outlying districts, were ultimately under the jurisdiction of the military authorities, though the civil authorities had some say in their government, and Europeans could acquire property there, but only within fixed limits. The Arab territory was reserved for the natives and only under very special and exceptional conditions were Europeans allowed to settle there at all.

Bugeaud's plan worked very satisfactorily from 1841 to 1847, when it was thrown out by the Chamber of Deputies and he re-signed. Before any new plans could be brought in, the February Revolution of 1848 took place, and the founding of the Republic; then followed the second Revolution of June, and the new con-stitution of October 1848.

One of the first acts of the new Republic was to declare Algeria an integral part of metropolitan France, without taking the time to discover—or indeed having the knowledge to decide—whether the policy would suit the stage of development of the colony. Each of the provinces was now divided into 'départements', each with a 'chef-lieu', a 'préfet', a 'conseil de préfecture' and a mayor. Outside this there was the military territory which sometimes overlapped with the civil territory, and this continued to be administered by the General commanding the Division in the province, and by the 'Bureaux Arabes', that is the section of the army which dealt with the natives, and the local Sheiks.

Luckily the conquest of Algeria had been achieved before the Revolution of 1848, as three different governors followed each other in quick succession during the three years of the Republic, each with different schemes for the development of the Colony. The country was peaceful it is true, but there was constant friction between the civil and military administration in each province, since their duties had not been clearly defined, nor the extent of their powers. There was also friction between the local administration and the home government. With these frequent alterations of policy and plan, seemingly unconcerned with the local well-being and thinking it of secondary importance, with these frequent changes of governor, no one ever knew what he could depend on, nor when everything was going to be upset and then started again from the very beginning.

A further difficulty which the administration and the inspectors had to contend with was that the settlers which the Republic was now sending out were of a very poor type, very different from Bugeaud's disciplined military or retired military colonists. They were, for the greatest part, men who could find no employment in France, those who had been thrown out of work by the closing of the 'Ateliers Nationaux', and those who had been implicated in the Revolution and were sent to North Africa as a prison sentence. They were mostly town-dwellers, as well as unwilling settlers, in poor condition physically and unsuited to the rough and primitive life in Africa. The majority of them were killed off by the cholera epidemics of 1849 and 1852.

Borel arrived in Algeria under Bugeaud's administration but he was only to serve under him for eighteen months. The greater part of his service however was spent in the subsequent period of mismanagement and disorder, when he got completely muddled between the various authorities. This eventually led to his disgrace for he had neither the tact nor the requisite kind of intelligence to steer an equal course between them. Had Bugeaud remained in Algeria as Governor he might well have avoided disaster, but then he would not have fulfilled his destiny, of which he wrote in *Madame Putiphar*, that of belonging to that category of men who are dedicated to misfortune.

Chapter 2

THE INSPECTOR

orel was stationed first in the town of Alger. His salary included an allowance for a horse, and was fixed at two thousand nine hundred francs a year, that is about one hundred and fifteen pounds. In his file preserved at the *Archives Nationales* in Paris he is stated to possess a private income of two thousand francs a year, and that would mean that he could count in all on a yearly income of some two hundred pounds. In Algeria where the cost of living was low and standards of life were simple, he would appear as almost well-to-do.

At first he seems to have liked his work and to have carried out his duties conscientiously and efficiently. He was happy in Alger and enjoyed a certain amount of pleasant social life. He was a constant guest at the house of the widow of a teacher from the Ecole de Commerce in Paris, called Antoinette Claye, who had a young son and a daughter of nineteen with whom Petrus Borel fell in love and whom he eventually married. It is not clear whether he met the family for the first time in Alger, or whether he had known them earlier in France. Both Aristide Marie and Claretie declare that he knew them first after his arrival in North Africa, but they are often so wrong in their details, that one cannot place reliance on what they say. They are certainly wrong when they state that he had a son shortly after his marriage, whereas this child was born ten years afterwards and indeed two years after his dismissal from service, in 1857. A letter from Borel's widow, written in 1868 to Théophile Gautier, seeking his support to obtain a free place for her son at the Lycée of Alger, makes this clear.[1] J. L. Audin claims, though he does not give his evidence for this statement, that Antoinette Claye had been a former mistress of Borel in Paris and that she accompanied him with her children when he went to Algeria. He suggests that Borel's marriage to her daughter was a 'mariage à trois'.[2] Madame Borel's letter to Gautier would seem to support Audin's contention that she had known him in Paris before he went into exile. Her letter is however not perfectly clear.

When Borel had been six months in the service the reports on him to the authorities were favourable, although it was also stated that he could, with advantage, show more energy in the discharge of his duties. 'Monsieur Borel is an artist, he likes the country and enjoys especially the duties which take him there most frequently. He devotes perhaps too much poetic feeling to his duties, but, apart from this tendency, which will eventually disappear in presence of practical reality, he is an able servant whose work is useful.'[3] The report adds that his style is more literary than official. This statement is probably what gave rise to the rumour, repeated by Claretie, that his reports were written in verse. They are all preserved in the *Archives Nationales* in France, all are in prose, and long-windedness and a high falutin' style are more evident than poetic expressions.

In 1847 Borel wrote an article called 'Algérie, Colonisation', and published it in *La Revue de l'Orient et de l'Algérie* in August that year, but it consists merely in the repetition of the material already furnished to the authorities in his terminal reports.

In July 1847 the authorities decided to move him from Alger to Mostaganem in the province of Oran, about a mile and a half from the sea. He was entrusted with the task of making a study of the district and of superintending the development of the concessions already granted to settlers.

Mostaganem was in a new and scarcely developed territory and there, for the first time, Petrus Borel felt really free and full of hope for the future. He thought that he would be able there to strike his roots and build a permanent home to which he could bring his bride. He was granted a concession and he determined to farm it in his spare time. His land lay in 'mixed territory'.

In September he returned to Alger on leave and married Gabrielle Claye. He brought her back with him to Mostaganem, with his mother-in-law and her young son. They were to help him to develop and farm his land. With the help of his mother-in-law's capital he built a house on his estate, the kind of house he had always dreamt of building, one designed by himself, a gothic mansion built of stone, suitable as a habitation for a Romantic poet, and characteristically called Castel de la Haulte Pensée.[4] Audin, who on a recent visit to Algeria went to see it, says that it is a bizarre construction with a square romantic tower, and that it is not without style.[5] It must however look strange indeed in the midst of the Algerian 'brousse'. The house now belongs to an architect who has restored it, and says that at night queer noises are heard in it, that doors securely locked at dusk are found open again the the morning. It would be right and fitting that the ghost of the Lycanthrope should haunt the castle which he himself had built, especially as Audin tells us that letters and documents which were found in a hole in a wall by the builders, were then destroyed by them.

At the end of 1847 the report on Borel's work is colourless and does not say very much. 'Character good!' it states 'Official conduct good! Private conduct very good! Manners good! Would he be more suitably employed in another post? I think not! He seems to have some ability and to be willing.'

By 1848 however he was beginning to cause anxiety and to incur blame. By this time Bugeaud had been gone a year and the resulting confusion had taken place which led to slackness in all but the most conscientious officials. Perhaps Borel was now spending too much time working on his own concession; it is certain that his official work now bored him and that he found it irksome. A report of March 1848 complained that, although he had occupied his present post for more than four months, he had furnished no reports of his activities, nor any statement of the deductions which he had drawn from his observation. The military authorities requested the civil authorities to see that this inspector fulfilled more conscientiously his duties as they were prescribed in the regulations.

One senses a certain sharpness of tone here, the touchiness of one government department in addressing another. The report indicates the clash between the civil and military authorities which resulted from the recent orders of the new Republic.

Whether the civil authorities obeyed the request of the military authorities is not known, but Borel persisted in omitting to furnish his reports and, in June, in company with several other equally inefficient inspectors, he was dismissed from the service.

His dismissal was not, at first, accepted by the home government; the Minister for War wrote to Algeria, 'I hear of the dismissal of Messrs Borel, Bornier, Lavaud and de Chanal, who do not appear to possess the necessary ability or knowledge to give satisfactory service and who, in fact, have given no service at all, as my predecessors have put on record on several occasions. I request you nevertheless to try to discover whether they could not be employed in other appointments where they might be more useful'[6]

Borel remained unemployed for a year. He did not attribute his dismissal to his inefficiency or his inadequacy as a civil servant, but solely to the grudge which he alleged that Armand Marrast, the former editor of *Le National*, had against him, and with whom he had clashed before he came to Algeria, and who was now a member of the new Republican government. Marrast had sent one of his officials to Algeria and the first action of this envoy had been to ratify the dismissal of the inspectors who had had unfavourable reports, amongst whom was Borel.[7]

Borel's attempt at retaliation was characteristic of him. A friend of the envoy was a candidate for election to the local government in Alger, and Borel, thinking thus to take vengeance on Marrast, wrote a satire against the candidate and sent it to the editor of the local paper for publication, but the latter, fortunately, had the good sense not to print it.

During the year when he was without employment, Borel lived at Haulte Pensée with his family and tried to eke out a living from his land. Then, in May 1849, he applied for reinstatement, claiming that his dismissal had been solely due to the socialist government which had resulted from the first revolution of 1848, and declared that he had been victimised on account of his political opinions. Petrus Borel, the ardent republican of 1830, was now in 1848 a fanatical reactionary. That was, as a matter of fact, in keeping with his character, since he could never support any government in power, and, as there was now a republican government in office, he was in opposition to it.

'Monsieur le Ministre' he wrote[8] 'Please permit me to bring my humble desires to your notice and to lay my request before you, to express how great would be my joy if it would be possible of your kindness to appoint me to the post of civil commissioner. The great attachment that is shown to me at Mostaganem by the inhabitants of the district, and the constant interest which the whole population has given me in the past and is still giving me in my retirement, lead me to the conclusion that I have been useful, just and honest in the fulfilment of my duties as Inspector of Colonisation, and that I should equally well carry out those of the new post for which I am applying. It is now twelve months since I was dismissed during the first troubled days of the Republic. I have borne this blow with resignation and, until today, in silence. But, Monsieur le Ministre, if you could think fit to put an end to the uncertainty of my position, you would be performing a good and generous action, and one which would have the happiest results on my future, and one for which my heart would always cherish beautiful and everlasting gratitude.

After saying this please allow me to close my request and not to insist any further, in the hope that Monsieur le Maréchal, Duc d'Isly, in whose service I was as inspector, will be kind enough to speak on my behalf and to support my respectful and rightful claim.'

Nothing happened for several months and then, at the end of 1849, supported by the Duc d'Isly, he was appointed to a post at Bône in the province of Constantine, the one at Mostaganem being already filled, and his salary was raised to one hundred and fifty pounds a year.

Borel was, however, not happy at Bône; his work worried him as he was tossed backwards and forwards between the civil and military administrations, and he never knew which orders were the most important for him to obey. When he had been there for six months, he wrote to General Daumas, who had always been kind and sympathetic to him, imploring him to get him sent back to Mostaganem. The letter is very characteristic of his official style; characteristic also are his accusations against all his colleagues, his indictment of their honesty and efficiency. 'Mon Général' he wrote[9] 'My friend de Chancel[10] and my supporter Monsieur le Gal de Saint Amant have, I am sure, written to you on my behalf, to beg you to be so kind as to send me back to Mostaganem. Indeed that is my dearest and sole wish, and since these gentlemen have kindly undertaken to put my modest request before you, that poor little ambition of mine, indeed so modest a request that if it were granted to anyone else but me, it would seem only a humiliation, I venture to add my supplications to theirs, not in order to give them more weight, but solely in order to underline by a few words of my own, heartfelt and imploring, if indeed I can find any, the greatness in my eyes—or at least in my heart—of the favour which I hope from your generosity.

After Marshal Bugeaud left Algeria I was sent to Mostaganem and I remained there for three years—eighteen months on active service and eighteen months in reserve. Three years of exile— eighteen months of neglect—that is more than enough time to form habits and to become rooted in the land where one is cast. During this period my mother-in-law bought a concession of land in the district overlooking the sea on the road to Mazayran. She built there a sort of picturesque 'cordj'*, surrounded by fortifications, which is almost entirely constructed of stone, and at great expense. She wished to build this house in a secluded place so that it could be handed on to her children and become a family seat. It is there that my family has settled, composed of my young wife, her young brother and my mother-in-law. It is there that I long to return. With so sedentary and involved a situation it is impossible for these deserving women to accompany me. They would lose the little they possess without gaining anything in return, except loss of cast. To move about Africa in miserable conditions,

* 'Cordj' is the Arab word for a dwelling.

in the trail of an inspector, from camp to camp, from Mostaganem to Galba, from Sentia to Setif, and so forth, would be ruinous financially, without honour, and altogether impossible. When I received the order to proceed to the province of Constantine, a few months ago, I did so without hesitation; I obeyed with alacrity, hoping that this eager obedience and submission to the decisions of my superiors would be remembered favourably to me later, when they hear of them, and of my attachments and affections which make it impossible for me to leave.

De Chancel has told me not to look on the black side of things and I shall not allow you to see my desperate longing, but I beg you, with clasped hands and on bended knees, not to leave me any longer in the painful situation in which I now find myself.

I have colleagues of my own standing who have never left Alger, nor gone to any other post since the body of inspectors was founded. Others, of more recent appointment, who have arrived from France and have not ventured, for even a day, beyond their port of disembarkation. As for me, I have been dragged all over Algeria, through all the three provinces. I know my Algeria through and through, from the sea to its most southern limits. There is little further for me to learn in that respect, and I have seen enough for purposes of comparison. If this experience has been valuable to me, it is completely lacking to my colleagues. If I am the only one amongst them who knows his French Africa thoroughly, and the only one who, by a combination of circumstances, is firmly rooted in one spot by interests deserving of consideration, by a *Smala** which cannot be moved, why should I have to wander eternally while my colleagues are allowed to crystallise in one spot? Why should I have to break up my *Penates*, my household Gods, whilst their furnished lodgings are forever respected.

I greatly fear that, in spite of the advice which de Chancel gave me, I have not hidden my grief from you! But you who have received from Heaven strength and generosity as your gifts, you cannot fail to be moved by my request, and to be just. You will forgive me, you will deign to forgive the weakness of my flesh,

*'Smala' is the Arabic word for household.

and I do not doubt that, although nothing has hitherto brought me to the notice of your kindness, you will pay some attention to the request which those who love me are making on my behalf, and which I present to you most humbly. Your decision will certainly have the greatest influence on the future which is in store for me. My fate—nay my whole life—hangs on your yea or nay. It is not however thus with my admiration and my gratitude, with my devotion to you; these are yours already, and these I shall always have the honour of expressing to your person, and they will certainly not depend on your answer—whatever it may be.

I have the honour of remaining, with the greatest respect, your submissive and obedient servant, Petrus Borel.'

It was not possible to do anything for him for another twelve months, but a comparatively favourable report on his work was received in July 1851, and this supported his request. It stated that he was excellently educated, that he spoke Spanish, English and Arabic fluently. It added 'Monsieur Borel is cold and distant in manner. He enjoys his work but does not like to bestir himself physically. His interest is sustained only for important work. He is somewhat thin-skinned and easily offended. He finds it difficult to fit in with the two forms of administration to which he is attached—civil and military—and that is why he would prefer to return to Mostaganem, where he has been obliged to leave his family and his personal interests, and to be appointed either to an exclusively military or an exclusively civil territory.'

In October 1851 he was finally reinstated to his post at Mostaganem. His friend Ausone de Chancel had just been appointed to the secretariat of the Prefecture at Oran and he was able to support Borel's appeal.[11] In the same month de Chancel himself was appointed as sous-préfet at Mostaganem.

Unfortunately an extremely unfavourable report followed Borel from Bône, which said that he had not furnished his reports before he left, although he had had ample time to do so. It was requested that he should be severely reprimanded.

'Monsieur Petrus Borel has consistently refused to furnish the work he has been asked to do by the civil authorities and in this he is like many of his colleagues. The result is that I can send you no report from his district.'[12]

As Borel had been responsible to two different authorities not much heed was paid to this report. He settled down happily at Mostaganem in the midst of his family and, for a time, won favourable reports from his superiors. In 1852 his report stated that he deserved promotion. He was said to be frank and loyal, to behave perfectly towards his superiors and that, as well as being an inspector, he had been elected Mayor of Bled Toccaria and that, in carrying out the duties of that office, he had shown ability and great devotion. 'The inhabitants of Bled Toccaria will never forget' the report added 'what he did for them during the difficult times that they had to undergo'. This was during the cholera epidemic of 1852. He built ovens to bake bread, stables and hen-houses; he founded a dispensary and even a school which soon counted eighty pupils. He created local industries which still flourish today, and he, the 'mangeur de curés' of 1830, even built a temporary chapel. When times grew worse he took on himself the responsibility of buying grain for bread out of public funds, saying that he did not hesitate to assume the responsibility, that he would do the same thing again in similar circumstances, for he could not sit back and watch, with folded hands, the population die of hunger whom it was his duty not only to lead but also to save, as far as he could, from the extremes of distress and even death. There were many who were saved by him, and Audin tells us of a family today that holds the name of Borel in veneration, because he had looked after their grandfather as an orphan child, when he was Mayor of Bled Toccaria.[13]

The figure of the Lycanthrope appears here with a grandeur that matches his more showy splendour of 1830. He was, as Audin says, trying to make real an Eden on earth, the Eden of his dreams, and to make of colonisation something more than mere exploitation.

Unfortunately for him in June 1852 Bled Toccaria was attached to the Commune of Aboukir, and he ceased to administer it.

Deprived of his mayoral office Borel began to grow weary and his zeal towards his duties slackened, so that by 1853 he was again deserving of censure. Unfortunately at the same time his friend and supporter de Chancel left Mostaganem to take up an appointment at Blidah, and he was replaced at the sous-préfecture at Mostaganem by the Vicomte de Gantès who was to become the chief instrument in bringing about the final disgrace and dismissal of Petrus Borel.

Chapter 3

DECLINE AND FALL

———————————◆◆◆◆◆◆◆————————————

Had Bugeaud remained Governor of Algeria, and had there not existed the constant rivalry and jealousy between the two departments administrating the country, Petrus Borel might have been able to pass unobserved in the crowd, like many another idle and inefficient agent. But he who, at the best of times, was an indifferent civil servant, consciously or unconsciously took advantage of the discord reigning between the officials, to do nothing at all. The result was that he was used as the obvious and Heaven-sent scapegoat on whose score each department could seek to discredit and attack the other. All this only drove him into fits of exasperation, but did nothing to improve his work. All through 1853 constant complaints were sent in against him for not having furnished his reports; or when, on the rare occasions he did send them in, the authorities declared that they were dissatisfied with their tone, and insisted on their being done again. Borel however, recalling his early fame as a writer, considered that, as a man of letters, he could be permitted to know how a mere report should be written. Yet it must be admitted that his long-winded, grandiloquent and pompous reports must have been entirely useless for the purpose for which they were intended, namely to give information. He was unsuited to work in a subordinate capacity, for, at the slightest word of rebuke, he took immediate umbrage, and his arrogance and truculence of 1830 used to break out, as he declared that he would allow no one to dictate to him. Yet, had he met with sympathy and understanding—as he had done in the time of Bugeaud

—had he received wise and tactful treatment, disaster might have been averted. But he became merely the pretext for disagreement between two government departments and, feeling that he was receiving some support from one side, he made no attempt to adapt himself to circumstances or to fulfil his duties. He was on particularly bad terms with de Chancel's successor as sous-préfet at Mostaganem. Borel had come to regard Mostaganem as his own private province and thus considered de Gantès as an interloper. Never was his lack of psychological insight—apparent also in his novels—more evident than in his dealings now with his colleagues and chiefs.

On 25th May it was put on record that a series of complaints had been made against him for repeated insolence towards de Gantès, and for refusal to perform the duties prescribed for him. On 29th July there was a further report which said that even when he did furnish his reports they were not those that he was requested to draw up. He had been merely asked to give a statement of fact but he had taken it upon himself to criticise the whole system of administration. 'I cannot tolerate' wrote the Préfet of Oran to his second in command the Sous-Préfet at Mostaganem, Monsieur de Gantès,[1] 'that an agent should deviate from the regulations to the extent of setting himself up as a censor. And so I have the honour of requesting you to inform Monsieur Borel that he must henceforth abstain from all critical observations in his reports. He is to content himself with giving the bare facts without endeavouring to attribute blame to agents who have preceded him and who, in his opinion, have hindered the development of colonisation.'

On 7th September 1853 Borel was fined eighty-five francs for carelessness in drawing up his statistical reports. A week later an adverse report was sent in about him on the score of a serious error in calculating the remuneration due to the labourers who had been clearing the bush. While the final report for the year stated: 'I have never been able to extract from Monsieur Borel any work at the correct and stated time. I must however add in his defence that, during the last quarter, he was given important duties to perform either by the General or else by the Préfet, which have distracted him from his regular work. I think however that, with a little more assiduity and willingness, Monsieur Borel could have achieved more. Nevertheless the frequent rebukes these delays have called forth have only soured and discouraged this agent who is intelligent and capable and who, in his own line, can be useful.' The report adds that his slackness in clerical work would always be a source of trouble, and it suggests that it would be advisable to place him in a post with less writing involved.

The following year Borel did a very foolish and ill-advised thing. Thinking that the military department was on his side against the civil administration, he took it upon himself to write directly to the Minister of War in Paris, to complain of the treatment to which he was subjected at the hands of the local civil authorities. 'Monsieur le Ministre' he wrote,[2] 'You will, I trust, deign to forgive the liberty I take in applying directly to you and in bringing to your notice the two enclosures, but no other course is open to an unfortunate man who is being driven to the brink of utter despair.' The two enclosures were, firstly a copy of the letter of complaint which the Préfet had sent to the Sous-Préfet on the manner in which he drew up his reports; and secondly a copy of the answer which he himself had sent to the Sous-Préfet. The answer had obviously been composed with a view to its being seen by other eyes than those of its recipient. It had been written expressly for the purpose of being forwarded to the Minister of War. It is a touchy and arrogant letter written in a style bordering on hysteria. 'An inspector' he wrote, 'naturally uses his reports to report. He does his duty and does not deliberately dig up things in order to report them. He carries out inspections and, when he carries out inspections as I carry them out, he does them thoroughly and conscientiously, and should earn the respect and praise of his superiors.' Then, in the midst of his official statement, he breaks into an impassioned and personal appeal which his relations with Monsieur de Gantès certainly did not warrant. It is obviously addressed to the Minister of War. 'I beg and implore you, Monsieur le Sous-Préfet, to descend to my level. Have the kindness to do me the honour of recognising the kind of servant I am, the kind of agent you have in your service, and you will realise how humiliating such remonstrations are to a man gifted with common-sense and with devotion to duty, whose chief merit is his power of observation, which faculty has never been placed in doubt, and who, by means of this gift, has enabled us, in the little commune of Mostaganem, to recognise and to bring to the notice of the authorities the nature of the cotton-plant.' Then follows a list of the many products which he claims to have discovered in North Africa. 'In the name of what Algerian science' he continues, 'in the name of what personal and local investigation do they presume to say that my knowledge is faulty, or that my investigations lack details. The facts set down by a man of research and integrity are facts to be accepted and nothing more.' Then follow pages of further grievances and he continues again, 'I wish to know, Monsieur le Sous-Préfet, whether the new Minister for War intends that this "hargnerie"—the expression is from Jean-Jacques*—should take the place, under his auspices, of the noble kindness, the august intelligence, which are normally the finest ornaments of the metropolitan administration. I am sending him a copy of the telegram and this letter without prejudice to the despatch of a full account of my tribulations during 1853. It is right, it seems to me, that his Excellency should at least realise how much gall is added to the bread of able and devoted agents.'

Such a letter was not calculated to ease the situation between the Sous-Préfet and Petrus Borel, especially now that the Minister for War was to be involved. On this letter can be seen, in the handwriting of the latter, jotted notes which say that it seems to him that Monsieur Borel is unduly touchy. 'I can see nothing in the categorical and precise requests sent to him by the Sous-Préfet to reduce him to such a state. In any case the complaints which he addresses to the Sous-Préfet are in exceedingly bad taste.'

Monsieur de Gantès, on being warned by Borel of his intention of writing to the Minister, wrote on his own account, enclosing Borel's report, a copy of his own complaints, and a copy of Borel's letter which the Minister had already received. To these papers he added a report composed by himself on Borel's behaviour as a civil servant, in which he drew up a list of his delinquencies: his

* Jean-Jacques Rousseau.

delays in producing his reports which were only sent in after frequent reminders, and then were so carelessly drawn up that they all had to be done again. The Inspector, he complained, had not only been negligent in his work, but—what was worse in the opinion of the Sous-Préfet—had been inspired by excessive vanity, and by a deplorable tendency towards aggressive statement, and he showed altogether a spirit of independence and insubordination which was dangerous to the running of the service. One of his reports—declared the Sous-Préfet—was couched in terms so abusive to the higher authorities that it had to be completely rewritten. He ended by saying that the administration of the colony would become perfectly impossible if all agents were permitted to be so independent and insubordinate in their behaviour as Monsieur Borel.

In March, Borel wrote again to the Minister complaining of the manner in which he was being badgered—nay even persecuted—on the score of his terminal reports. His letter is a wordy document in which he explains to the Minister—who realised this fact perfectly himself—the purpose for which the reports of the inspectors had originally been devised. In Borel's view they were intended to set forth the opinions of the inspectors, it therefore followed that the Sous-Préfet had been wrong when he had tried to alter the work of the inspector and to substitute his own personality for that of the agent. The work of each inspector, according to Borel, should reach the Ministry for War in the form in which it had been drawn up. He declared that, to subscribe to the wishes of the Sous-Préfet would be to sign the death-warrant of the corps of inspectors, and he felt it his duty to defend that body to which he had the honour of belonging. If the inspectors were merely to provide statistics then he thought that these could more easily and more cheaply be obtained from municipal clerks and that it was useless and extravagant to employ more highly paid and experienced inspectors for that work.

Theoretically there was naturally a great deal of truth in Borel's contention, it was only unfortunate that it should be voiced by himself. General Daumas obviously considered that there was something in what he was saying, and also, as a military man and

in charge of the Division in Algeria, he was inclined to be unsympathetic to the civil administration. So, when appealed to,
he spoke in Borel's defence to the Minister. He said that he could
not help feeling that there might be a grain of truth in some of the
complaints of the unfortunate inspector who was being need-
lessly badgered. He too, he said, was of the opinion that the
reports of the inspectors were intended to inform the authorities
in Paris of the state of affairs in Algeria, and that they ought not
to be tampered with by any of the local authorities who wished to
give their own picture of conditions. He, for his part, considered
that it was Borel's duty to draw attention to any abuses which he
might see, and which could then be righted. He admitted however that Borel left much to be desired as an agent in the fulfilment of his duties, and added that there would be no injustice in
informing him that, if he did not henceforth become more
punctual and conscientious in his work, severe measures would
be enforced against him. 'I should however like' he ended 'to
request that some consideration should be shown to this inspector,
that his work and his style should not be the object of niggling
criticism, and that he should be reprimanded only for serious
lapses.'

Borel, feeling that he was now being supported by the military
authorities, and that no sanctions would be taken against him, was
becoming more truculent and insubordinate than ever. During
the whole of 1854 the complaints against him continued as bitter
as ever. He was accused of dangerous exaggeration when, in one
of his reports, he stated that the population of Sidi Cherif and
Aboukir was composed only of lazy and inefficient settlers who
should be evicted. The Sous-Préfet declared that, when he sought
for further information, he discovered that the inspector had been
unjust and that no reliance could be placed on his allegations. He
then asked the higher authorities to transfer Borel from Mostaganem, saying that he was a constant nuisance to the administration. General Daumas was again questioned and once more took
Borel's part, saying that, in his opinion, he had been made the
victim of a clash between the two sets of authority—civil and
military—and he declared that the local authorities did not always

behave towards him with the tact that they should, and that, by the sharpness of their recriminations they tended to aggravate the situation. His final conclusion was that the work of the Inspector had been subjected, on the part of the local authorities, to criticism which was often unjust. The Sous-Préfet was then requested by the Minister for War to deal more sympathetically and more gently with Borel. This did not tend to make him more acceptable to de Gantès. Writing to the Préfet, and enclosing one of Borel's reports, he said 'This pathetic lucubration of a bitter and diseased mind goes so far beyond anything that he has hitherto sent me, that I refuse to contradict all his falsehoods and all his spitefulness unless you command me to do so. I find it impossible to believe that it can ever have entered the mind of the home government to allow agents of this sort the right to turn their terminal reports into public indictments and to summon the local administration to the bar to defend its services'.

On receiving this letter the Préfet wrote again to Paris to request that Borel should be dismissed. The Minister for War was now beginning to be weary of the whole Borel problem, with which he had been plagued now for more than two years. He was beginning to think that the Préfet and Sous-Préfet might be right after all when they asserted that he was more trouble than he was worth. He was now obliged to admit that there might be legitimate grounds for complaints against him—his slackness in furnishing his reports, his harshness to settlers, and his general insubordination. But, on the other hand, General Daumas had implanted in him the suspicion that some of Borel's grievances might be justified and that he was being baited by the local bureaucracy. He then informed the Préfet that it was not the intention of the Government that treatment wounding to the dignity of an Inspector should be meted out to him, as it might easily make him lose all interest in his work. He wrote also to the Governor of Algeria, and insisted that Borel was to be given complete liberty of action in the matter of drawing up his reports. He said that it was his opinion that Borel was more discouraged than neglectful, and that, after having reviewed the matter once more from the beginning and thinking of previous cases, he had come to the considered conclusion that the local authorities might not always have behaved in a just and sympathetic manner to this very difficult Inspector, and that their actions had contributed much towards embittering and souring 'cet esprit déjà malade et bien préoccupé'. He was anxious he concluded that no immediate step should be taken to increase the state of agitation into which Borel had fallen.[3]

It must be admitted that Borel met with nothing but kindness and consideration from the Metropolitan authorities, and that the Minister for War particularly, helped by the information which he had received from General Daumas, reached a sound estimate of the Inspector's state of mind.

As de Gantès could no longer hope to have Borel transferred elsewhere, he complained to the Préfet that he was obliged, if he did not wish to be hamstrung in his duties, to employ clerks from his own office to do the work which Borel ought to have performed. He asked to be relieved from all responsibility for obtaining reports from him and for permission to employ a clerk permanently to do this work. Having obtained this permission, his next step was to try to have Borel retired as redundant, or else transferred to another station where he might be employed. He wrote to the Préfet,[4] 'This agent who spends his entire life in doing nothing at all, will not alter his behaviour of refraining from work, in which habit he is now deeply set this long time. You must realise, Monsieur le Préfet, how insulting and humiliating to me such behaviour is. I have never encountered another example of such open and prolonged insubordination against authority, without its receiving well-deserved retribution.'

There is little doubt that Borel's truculence and arrogance, his growing persecution mania, were signs of his becoming mentally deranged. He had now only one preoccupation in his head, and that was to bring about the ruin of his arch-enemy the Sous-Préfet, Monsieur de Gantès. He thought of nothing else. But only a man with a decided mental kink could have gone to the lengths to which he finally went. Matters reached a crisis when definite action had to be taken against him. His accusations were no longer confined to the administration in general, but were levelled against certain individuals in particular in the local administration, and these accusations were so outrageous that they could no longer be overlooked and received with silent contempt. They had to be investigated and accepted, or else refuted. The matter had to be once and for all cleared up.

Chapter 4

THE DEATH OF THE WOLF

———————————·:·-·:·+·:·+·i·⊕·i·+·:·+·:·-·:·———————————

Petrus Borel continued to believe that the Vicomte de Gantès cherished a grudge against him, and was working to obtain his dismissal. Then, seeking a reason for his alleged spite against himself, he came to the conclusion that the Sous-Préfet went in fear of him, terrified of what he might disclose of his malpractices during his administration. With the thoroughness of a maniac Borel set himself the task of discovering what he considered damaging evidence against his chief. Later, at the enquiry into Borel's accusations, it transpired that he had tramped round the country collecting gossip and slander to build up his indictment, all of which he believed implicitly without verification, just as he had elicited it from idle wastrels who were ready to slander others provided that they were not obliged to substantiate their statements on oath in a court of law, ready to say anything for the sake of a free drink. At last, when he thought he had collected sufficient evidence with which to hang the Sous-Préfet, Borel sent a report to the Préfet entitled 'How all co-operation is rendered impossible and ridiculous for the Inspector of Colonisation'. In this he complained that all his reports reached the Ministry in Paris misrepresented and distorted. He said that de Gantès was seeking his ruin, and he demanded that his original reports should be produced or he would apply directly to the Minister for War for redress. Then followed a grandiloquent passage in true Borellian style. 'And, so long as the Minister for War has not broken my career, and my life, I shall not suffer any longer anyone to deprive me of my rightful prerogatives and duties. It is a clumsy and despicable piece of diplomatic tactics to proceed, as has been done here, to get the work of a special agent done by someone else, and then to accuse him of refusing to obey, of being an idler who is unwilling to do anything and with whom nothing can be done.'[1]

Had matters rested here it might all have been dismissed as another of mad Borel's exaggerations, and nothing more need have been said about it. But he was not content with stopping at that. Seeking an explanation for de Gantès' spite against himself, he attributed it wholly to the alleged fact that the Sous-Préfet was afraid of him, afraid that he might divulge all that he had uncovered of his malpractices. He accused him of having, on several occasions, pocketed public funds, and the terms in which these accusations were couched left the authorities no option but to take action. 'And what is the origin of this hatred, this spite, of this fierce animosity against a poor little Inspector of Colonisation, of the lowest category, in his nature so calm and inoffensive?' asked Borel, 'animosity and rage which set everything in motion against me—calumny of all kinds, abuse, lies, foul slander —witness the libel drawn up by Monsieur Quesnel, the grand panjandrum of the Sous-Préfet and of colonisation, signed de Gantès, which accompanies my terminal reports. But why this hatred foaming at the mouth? It is easy, Monsieur le Préfet, to explain it! It is that I am in the way. I am honest and above-board, and I do not therefore give satisfaction. They need a rogue and an accomplice! The base envy and base spite of his Lordship Quesnel against Monsieur Petrus Borel are moreover fed by the evident repulsion which he inspires in me. What can I do! What can anyone do! He is a crook! And I cannot overcome the disgust which thieves and scoundrels inspire in me! At first, and on several occasions, I tried to explain to Monsieur le Vicomte de Gantès that it was painful and difficult for me to collaborate with his Colonisation Office, that my work would certainly be distressing to me as long as I was obliged to endure the contacts which honour forbids me to suffer. But Monsieur de Gantès always refuses to listen to me. I say to myself then that he must be very ill-informed if he does not know what goes on around him, in his very own office, under his orders and under his auspices, then he is a very poor and incompetent head. But if he knows everything and does not denounce it, then he is a great scoundrel, a boss who is obliged to aid and abet his subordinates. When I said this to myself I was doubly right, for Monsieur de Gantès is in fact a poor and incompetent head, his miserable administration proves that. On the other hand he is a great scoundrel because he is a boss who turns a blind eye to the shameful doings of a subordinate so that this subordinate should, in return, lend himself to his culpable actions and not give the show away. And how, Monsieur le Préfet, do you imagine that Monsieur de Gantès can have a restraining and improving influence on Monsieur Quesnel, his accomplice, his representative as Head of the Office of Colonisation, when he himself has acted as follows.'[2] Then Borel enumerates under four headings his accusations against the Sous-Préfet. Firstly that he pocketed the proceeds from the sale of trees from the government estates. Secondly that he pocketed the proceeds from the public Ball held in aid of the districts stricken by the cholera. Thirdly of having made out a false expenses account for the Ball held on the Feast of the Assumption, and of having pocketed the sum returned. And finally of having intrigued for the dismissal of Monsieur Petrus Borel when the latter uncovered his malpractices.

On receiving this letter the Préfet sent it to Paris to the Ministry for War, and the Minister finally decided that the matter must be investigated and cleared up. Writing to the Governor of Algeria he said,[3] that although he was convinced that there could be no vestige of truth in Borel's allegations, they impugned too directly the honour of the Sous-Préfet for the matter to be ignored, and that they must be ventilated and settled one way or the other, through a thorough investigation. He said that if Monsieur Borel's accusations were false then this should be clearly established, and the Inspector severely dealt with. If, on the other hand, they were true then Monsieur de Gantès was not a fit or proper person to hold an important government post. He therefore requested the Governor of Algeria to hold an enquiry and to clear up the matter once and for all.

Whatever may be the truth concerning Borel's allegations against de Gantès, there is little doubt that his action was, from his own point of view, extremely foolish. He was a very inefficient civil servant who owed his tenure of office to the leniency of the home authorities, and to the fact that they did not entirely trust the fair-mindedness and sense of justice of the local administration. If a public enquiry were set on foot, then all Borel's delinquencies would be brought out into the open by his opponents and exaggerated. Even if de Gantès were guilty of what he was accused of, Borel would have no chance against him. He had opportunities for bribing witnesses denied to his subordinate, for he handled ample funds, whereas Borel was poor and had no money at his disposal. He was any way too honourable to use public funds in this way. The local settlers, many of whom were scoundrels, would certainly realise that it was to their better interest to support an influential official like de Gantès, rather than an irresponsible eccentric such as Borel. De Gantès would remember those who supported him, and, even if he were guilty, he was certain of getting off scot free; while, on the other hand, if he had been maligned, he had nothing to fear either. He was bound to win in either case.

The enquiry was set on foot and lasted from 28th May until 10th June 1855, but the findings of the Court were only made public on 12th August.

It is impossible now to unravel the truth, or to discover whether there were any grounds for Borel's accusation against his superior. He brought forward no legal evidence to support his allegations, and they seem to have been built up merely on market-square and tavern gossip—whether true or false is not clear—on facts which he had elicited, and then exaggerated out of all proportion. But, even if he had no evidence of legal value, his allegations may still have been true nevertheless. A study of the voluminous set of documents brought forward by de Gantès leaves one with the suspicion that his supporters may well have been lying—they had ample opportunity to do so with impunity. They certainly never refuted Borel's accusations, but only concentrated their efforts on establishing that he had no proof. All the witnesses on whom Borel had counted left him in the lurch at the last moment, and would not swear in Court to what he had declared they had asserted to him. And he himself, with his eccentric and wild manner, inspired no confidence in those who were investigating his allegations. It must also be admitted that the enquiry was conducted in a manner unsympathetic to him, and gave him no chance, if indeed he ever had one. The local authorities would naturally prefer the immolation of Borel to the unmasking of de Gantès even if he were guilty—it would be far less troublesome in the long run for all concerned, and less likely to lead to further enquiries.

De Gantès stated in his defence that the trouble had started through Borel's vanity. He said that under his predecessors the Inspectors had been assuming more and more power, so that, when he was appointed, he had decided to keep them strictly within the limits of their rightful functions. This, he said, seemed to annoy Borel, whose pride was wounded—as had been evident in his defence when he had stated that 'Monsieur de Gantès did not remember that my position as Inspector gave me very import-ant and real prerogatives. He took me for a subordinate and ended by being impertinent to me'. De Gantès then went on to elabo-rate how, for two years previous to the present trouble, he had been obliged to complain continually to the authorities about the delinquencies of Borel, of his slackness in carrying out his duties, of his refusal to furnish his reports at the stated time, and of his accusations against all and sundry whenever he did produce any reports. Matters had become so serious that he had been even-tually obliged to request the Préfet to relieve him of all responsi-bility with regard to the work entrusted to Borel. All this he had borne with patience and endurance, but now it was different when the allegations were being directed against his private character, and he felt that he must insist on the matter being cleared up and his name exonerated. Borel was then summoned to state his case. He started badly and alienated sympathy by declaring that he did not wish to be interrogated in the Sous-Préfecture as that locality might be prejudicial to him, and because his witnesses might feel intimidated there. The Court however declared that it was the only place available in the district, and that the enquiry could hardly be held in the hotel. In his declaration Borel declared that, since his return to Mostaganem, he had been the object of constant spite on the part of the Sous-Préfet, and that the only explanation he could find for this state of affairs was that his superior wished to obtain his dismissal, because he knew too much of what was going on. De Gantès also wished him out of the way, he said, because he wanted to give his post to one of his minions. He accused him further of altering and cutting his reports. But, when this last allegation was investigated, it proved to be a misstatement. Borel had declared that a report of thirty or forty pages had been rewritten in the Sous-Préfecture. When however it was produced it turned out to be a document consisting of only ten pages to which the Sous-Préfet had appended explanatory notes. Borel was then asked to state what other reports of his had been tampered with, but could recall none. De Gantès then answered that the only reports which had been prepared at his office were those which Borel had obstinately refused to produce. Nevertheless some reports must have been kept back for none of those complained of earlier by the Sous-Préfet were to be found in the files of the trial, nor are they amongst the other papers at the Archives Nationales dealing with the Inspectors of Colonisation.

Borel next accused de Gantès of not having gone up to Bled Toccaria during the cholera epidemic, and also Doctor Clauzel of having failed to give his patients proper care. To counterbalance this de Gantès was able to produce witnesses—honest or venial is not clear—who swore that Borel himself had never been near the place. Here Borel interrupted heatedly and exclaimed with great rhetoric: 'Damnable lie! Infamous calumny! Thus to attack my honour, my character, my priesthood! I can do no better than to leave the duty of avenging me in the hands of Monsieur le Ministre de la Guerre, but if Monsieur le Ministre should find the task too humble or unworthy of him, then I would beg the Conseil d'Etat for permission to prosecute Monsieur de Gantès independently of the law and the tribunals of the Empire.'

Next the whole Commission trekked up to Bled Toccaria to

investigate the matter on the spot. The Mayor of the village—bribed or not—stated categorically that Borel had only once been to the village to fetch something, and cannot have been more than a few hours there, since no one had seen him. By this time all seemed to have forgotten the part he had played when he was Mayor of Bled Toccaria three years before. As far as de Gantès was concerned, the Mayor added, nothing could have equalled his courage. Not only did he go into all the houses, but he himself tended the sick. This evidence has the stamp of all sycophantic evidence, it is over-done and over-zealous. 'We left Bled Toccaria' reported the Commission to the Governor General, 'utterly convinced of the truth of the accusations made against Monsieur Borel by the Sous-Préfet, and we cannot agree that this agent was speaking the truth when he declared that slurs had been cast on his 'priesthood'. No one thought of consulting the report which had been sent about Borel in 1852, when it had been stated that the inhabitants of Bled Toccaria would never forget all that he had done for them. Borel himself must not have known of its existence for he did not produce it as evidence in his own defence.

When the Court reached the question of Borel's accusations of dishonesty against the Sous-Préfet, they discovered that he could furnish no proof whatsoever to support his allegations. Those who, according to him, had given him the information, now stated on oath that they had no knowledge whatsoever of the matter. The Commission then decided that Borel had only been lying, and they were satisfied that he had not been able to substantiate any of his accusations. But they did not investigate the matter of the present whereabouts of the money in question. As one reads the evidence, one is left with the uncomfortable suspicion that there may well have been some jobbery in the Sous-Préfet's office, either by de Gantès himself, or else by his subordinates with his connivance. A cleverer man than Borel would have left that particular hornet's nest severely alone—unless he had the implements at his disposal with which to smoke it out. Audin[4] says that a few months later the culprits were unmasked and that Quesnel, who was the scapegoat for the lot, was condemned to prison for two years. He however does not give his evidence. By that time unfortunately it was too late to do anything for Borel.

De Gantès now retaliated by bringing a counter-charge against Borel, accusing him of embezzling money which should have gone to the settlers. Witnesses also stated that they had lost heavily in all their transactions because he had failed to produce the necessary papers at the correct time.

The Commission finally came to the conclusion that Borel's allegations against the Vicomte de Gantès were false down to their smallest details, and that the Sous-Préfet had the right to expect the fullest vindication and reparations for the wrong done to him—that is public exoneration and the dismissal of his slanderer. 'Our final opinion' they added 'is that Monsieur de Gantès is an honourable man who has been cruelly and grossly libelled by his subordinate, Monsieur Petrus Borel, Inspector of Colonisation.'

In the meantime, while awaiting the verdict, Borel, with his usual lack of sense of reality, refused to work with the Sous-Préfet until he had been promoted as a reward for his services, and until the Minister for War had recommended him for the decoration of Chevalier de la Légion d'Honneur.

The final verdict was however not favourable, it pronounced the dismissal of Borel, and, although it was not to be made public until some months later, he was informed of it confidentially by the Chairman of the Commission, Le Comte de Dax. In answer Borel wrote one of his most amazing diatribes, in which he informed the Count that the light of God would be withdrawn from him since he was about to condemn an innocent man. He went on to say that he pitied him for he himself believed in retribution, even here below on earth, and that the Count would suffer for the injustice he was about to commit. He seemed unable to grasp the fact that he was really being dismissed and dishonoured.

'Monsieur le Conseiller,' he wrote,* ' J'ai pris et je prends encore pour un dernier coup de sonde ce que vous m'avez dit en faisant,

*Letter 12th June 1855, quoted in the French to do full justice to his style.

sous l'apparence d'un avertissement officieux, savoir que je n'étais pas parvenu à faire pénétrer en vous une conviction favorable envers moi, c'est à dire envers la vérité, et que vous conclueriez à ma révocation. Mais si ce n'est là qu'un dernier moyen, rappeler celui du Roi-juge, employé pour arriver à entendre le cri de la vraie mère, s'il peut être réel que l'esprit saint vous ait retiré jusque là ses lumières, et que vous soyez en voie de vous méprendre si considérablement et de frapper à côté des coupables, je revendiquerai alors pour moi la peine que vous me disiez ressentir, et je vous plaindrai dans mon cœur! Car je crois en Dieu, et à l'expiation même sur la terre, et je concevrai cette certitude que vous serez châtié dès ici-bas pour votre jugement inique, en attendant que vous rendiez compte de votre prévarication dans un monde rémunérateur du sang d'Abel fumant pour la fronde et le dol, versé dans la coupe de la haine et de l'envie, épanché en manière de libation sur l'autel d'Hermès, ce faux dieu infâme, cette idole de tous les temps, cette déité des carrefours, des marchands et des voleurs.

Monsieur, on vous a envahi, on vous a étourdi, on vous a ahuri de clameurs et de tumultes, on a précipité sur vous toute la bande des hommes tarés ayant essayé la rigueur de ma probité, de mon caractère et de mes fonctions, tous les bas envieux, tous ceux qui convoitent violemment et depuis longtemps mon emploi, on a ouvert sur vous la porte du bestiaire, le vomitorium; on vous a livré à la canaille du pays, à la meute de mes ennemis pour vous faire tomber dans l'aveuglement. Mais laissez un peu les vagues de la calomnie soulevées autour de vous à propos de moi. Laissez un peu la mer agitée se rasseoir et le calme se faire, puis ensuite de nouveau plongez dans la profondeur des flots plus clairs et alors vos yeux se décelleront et liront dans la limpidité renaissante. La perle de la vérité étincellera sous vos regards étonnés dans son abri de nacre, au fond, tout au fond de l'abyme creusé par les méchants, et enfin peut-être un peu aussi par vous. Adieu, Monsieur, recevez mes félicitations pour le cas où vous feriez bonne et sévère justice, celle pour laquelle vous avez été envoyé par le Ministre de la Guerre et par le Gouverneur Général et celle que je vous ai prié de rendre au nom de Dieu. Du reste, Monsieur, ne comptez pas que je fasse bon marché de moi-même. Jamais! Tant qu'il y aura une goutte d'encre dans ma plume, une goutte de sang dans mes veines, je persisterai, je me défendrai! Un homme d'un caractère antique ne se rend pas, il faut le tuer pour le vaincre.—Petrus Borel d'Hauterive.'

Suffering gave Borel a magnificence of style he had not shown for a long time. This letter, in spite of its great length, in spite of its unsuitability for its recipient, is worthy to be included in an anthology of memorable letters. It is only at this time that Petrus Borel began to use the suffix of d'Hauterive to which he had no more right than his brother who had used it for many years. Up to 1855 Borel had done nothing to identify himself with the noble family of Borel d'Hauterive. Now, confronted by his enemy, Le Vicomte de Gantès, and the Chairman of the Commission, Le Comte de Dax, he gave in to the temptation to prove himself as noble as they, and signed his letters Petrus Borel d'Hauterive.

Matters took their course and Borel was finally dismissed from the service in August 1855.

After his dismissal he lived with his wife and family on his lands at Haulte Pensée. Writing to his brother, André Borel d'Hauterive who was in Paris, he informed him that he was no longer an Inspector.[6] 'I was dismissed because I refused to work with that scoundrel the Vicomte de Gantès, the Sous-Préfet of Mostaganem and his minion Q(uesnel), "un voyou, un marlou, un arsouille, un grinche."' He informed his brother that he had become a simple 'fellah' and that, with the help of his family, he was trying to live on the proceeds of his lands. In this cantankerous letter he complains that his brother is always lamenting his fate, as if he had anything to complain of. He, Petrus, is without books or papers of all sorts, and he begs his brother to send him some, a few even of those he has finished with.

He had not however lost all hope of being reinstated in his post of Inspector, and the following year he sent an application to the Minister for War, asking for reappointment.[7] 'Monsieur le Ministre' he wrote 'it is a year today since I was struck off and excluded from the Administrative Body by the order of your Excellency. I am still waiting for the reparation which is my due.

I have the honour of remaining, with deepest respect, the very humble and obedient servant of your Excellency. Petrus Borel d'Hauterive.'

This letter received no answer and deep depression settled on Borel. An echo of this is found in the only poem which we have from his pen after he went to Algeria, *La Léthargie de la Muse*, though we do not know its date. Perhaps the Muse which was sleeping in him was roused to song again at the news of the death of Gérard de Nerval one winter's night in 1855, who when he was penniless and cold hanged himself outside a doss-house which had refused him admission. Gérard de Nerval and he had been close friends in the days of the *Bouzingos*, when he, Petrus, had been the dashing young leader of the gay young band, and full of hope of a glorious future. Neither he nor Nerval had been able to acclimatise themselves to ordinary everyday life. Nerval had chosen the way of escape of Champavert, through suicide. But Borel, although still alive in body, was nevertheless dead as a poet. He had written no poetry since he had left France ten years before, and he had moreover nothing positive to show for his years of exile, for he was a prematurely aged man, without a settled position, and as poor as any native. His tribulations had only soured him, they had not burst out in song. Now the news of the tragic death of his old friend and comrade may have temporarily set free the spring of feeling so that it welled up in a poem which does not rank far below his finest poetry.[8]

In his last years in Algeria there was nothing left of the daring leader of 1830, who seemed to his friends like a Spanish grandee. Now, although he was not yet fifty, he looked a decrepit old Don Quixote, with his uncared-for grey beard, his bald pate, and working in the fields almost in rags like a tramp.

A son was born two years after his dismissal, in 1857, after ten years of marriage.[9] One would like to think that the birth of his heir brought some satisfaction and happiness to the old lycan-thrope. His names at least suggest family pride. They were: Aldéran-André-Petrus-Benoni Borel d'Hauterive. One can see in them that the old romantic had not yet died.

Petrus Borel died on 17th July 1859. Claretie says that it was of sunstroke, since he would never wear a hat or any covering for his bald pate in the heat of the desert sun. He himself used to declare that everything that God did He did well, and that if He intended that his head should be covered He would have left him his hair. Since he had none it meant that his head needed no protection. Nature does right what she does and it is not for us to interfere with her. Other writers say that he died of hunger, or that he was so much disgusted with everything, so revolted by the hideous injustice of the world that, like Champavert and like Gérard de Nerval, he refused to live any longer, allowing himself to die as a supreme protestation against life. Death of hunger, through poverty, in exile, would be an ending in keeping with the temperament and destiny of the lycanthrope. Houssaye says,[10] 'Hunger drives the wolves from the forests, but the poor lycanthrope, in the arid deserts of North Africa, was unable to find a single sheep to devour.'

The lycanthrope died, like a wolf, in a desolate land, far from his own country and his early friends.

According to Audin,[11] he was buried with religious rites in the parish cemetery at Mostaganem. Later this was put to other than burial uses, but no one thought of collecting his remains for re-interment elsewhere, so that no stone today marks his last resting place, and no one knows where the bones of the hapless lycanthrope have been cast away. This last degradation is the final symbol of that destiny blighted by 'le guignon'.

CONCLUSION

Posterity, on the whole, has not treated Petrus Borel kindly, nor has it ever given him his just deserts, whereas it has singled out for special praise many a lesser writer. He is now almost entirely forgotten, except amongst a small number of devotees who find the by-ways of literature often more absorbing than the highways. Even in his own lifetime he had become neglected as early as twenty years before his death, when his last published work, *Madame Putiphar*, which appeared in 1839, aroused so little enthusiasm.

Petrus Borel was the kind of meteoric personality who is thrown up by violent revolution, whose light burns brightly for a short space, as long as the fashion for destruction prevails, and then finally, because he cannot adapt himself to the conditions of stable society, splutters out into obscurity. He was, by nature and inclination, capable of destruction, but he never learned to build. Yet his stormy passage through his age has not been in vain, for he hewed out a rough channel which later writers—Baudelaire, Rimbaud and Lautréamont—have deepened for the greater glory of literature, and who owe much to him, who might indeed never have existed had it not been for his fulgent example.

Baudelaire was to see in Borel a man fatally persecuted by 'le guignon', a man blighted by the evil-eye, to whom the curse of God allowed no rest. This was Borel's conception of the destiny of all mankind. The reasons for this frustrated destiny in his own case are not far to seek. He lacked the breadth of genius to achieve his high ambitions, and yet was too proud to be satisfied with what his talents allowed him to be. It is evident from his writings that he did violence to his nature in his efforts to practise Sadism and Satanism. In cruelty his practice fell far below his promise. He was a man characterised by kind and warm sensibilities, whom the harshness of life wounded bitterly; he was unable to accept the conditions of life as he saw them, and his revolt was expressed in a deliberate pursuit of cynicism and brutality in his writings. Yet, underneath this bitter exterior, there beat the heart of a man moved by deep compassion for those who suffer and are ill-treated by their fellow-men—this is clear even in his most cruel book, *Madame Putiphar*. Houssaye, who knew Borel intimately as a young man, says, with some acumen,[1] that Borel was always cast for the wrong part, that he deliberately chose one for which he was least suited. He rewrote the part given to him by Nature in accordance with his taste. Houssaye goes on to say that he took infinite pains to cultivate red roses in his garden where white ones would have grown in profusion without effort or care. This would explain why his final achievement bore so little relation to his promise. Later, when the taste for melodrama had gone out of fashion, he wrote another part for himself, that of the academic scholar, and became a historian and a linguist. Ten years after his beginnings in the charnel-house literature of 1830, he was writing additional chapters for the *Essays of Montaigne*. Unfortunately the public did not want learning from him and gave him no encouragement.

Like Rostand's *Cyrano de Bergerac* Borel was often carried away by a love of the theatrical conception of 'la Gloire', by a liking for false 'panache'. This is apparent in his efforts to appear in a theatrical part as a writer, rather than in concentrating on what he was saying. He was always in fancy dress playing his part like a nineteenth-century actor of melodrama, and he could never cope with life as it is lived.

Borel's aspirations and personality are probably ultimately more interesting than his actual literary achievement. Right to the end of his life he remained, what he had been in his early days, an 'honnête homme' inspired by a bitter hatred of everything that was mean and low, by a horror of falsehood and dishonesty. He makes his hero Champavert say that the thought which arouses most disgust in himself is the fear that he—or anyone else—might

cease from being an honest man.[2] He himself made similar statements about his chiefs and colleagues in Algeria when he suspected them of malpractices. Even when his mind became mentally deranged, at the end, this characteristic still shone out, but
with a dark distorting light. This quality, although it made of him
a figure of fun when it was exaggerated, gave him nevertheless the
pathetic grandeur of a Don Quixote tilting against spiritual wind-
mills. He was inspired by generosity of outlook, a longing to
support those who were oppressed, but this eventually became
twisted and he ended by believing that the underdog was always
right, merely because he was the underdog. He had a bitter hatred
of everything that was vulgar or mean, and this eventually led to
his downfall and death.

Borel's personality led him often into intolerance, and he never
learned to have pity for the weaknesses of average humanity.
Average human nature was what he most loathed and despised.
Baudelaire's revulsion against the petty meannesses of men was
equal to his, but he felt however as well deep compassion, not
only for those who suffer and are ill-used at the hands of others,
but pity also for those who fail through their own weakness and
frailty. Borel's pity went only to the defenceless and persecuted,
but not to those who, seeing good, fail to reach it. He had not
sufficient self-criticism to realise how fatally easy it is to be weak
in attainment, nor how this failure cannot always be attributed to
others, but to oneself alone. He never studied or criticised himself
deeply and this led to arrogance which made him feel that he himself was incapable of sinking as low as those whom he despised.
He would never have said with Baudelaire:

> *Ah! Seigneur, donnez-moi la force et le courage*
> *De contempler mon cœur et mon corps sans dégoût.*

All writers are, in a certain measure, ego-centric by the very nature
of their craft, but Borel was turned in on himself in introspection
rather than in self-analysis. This lack of psychological analytical
power made him unsuited to be a novelist, but his quick sensibilities and feeling for atmosphere made him reach noble heights
in the short story. It is in this literary form that his chief fame as a

writer lies. In it his obsession with the depicting of torture and physical suffering, is more suitable than in a novel. In it too his mordant and ironical humour without a trace of laughter or fun, his 'humour noire', is seen to best advantage.

His poetry too is worthy of high mention, and, at its best, is inspired by a note of bitter suffering not yet encountered in French poetry. He composed also one long poem, the noble symbolism of which foreshadows that of Baudelaire.

In his person Petrus Borel was a living protest against the utilitarianism and materialism of the reign of Louis Philippe. He had a loathing and contempt for bourgeois values and, in an age when everyone was prostituting his talent for gain—even Gautier sold his soul for the easy money of ephemeral journalism at a time when the new reviews made this a lucrative occupation for those whose scruples were not too fine—he was unable to follow the example of his contemporaries. It requires all sorts of qualities— both good and bad—to be able to exploit one's talent for gain, and Borel possessed none of them.

Yet the literary soil fertilised by Borel's suffering, and watered by his bitter tears, was eventually to prove a richer one for posterity than that of any of his contemporaries or immediate successors, except Baudelaire, and all subsequent schools of poetry—Symbolist to Surrealist—found inspiration in his writings.

Petrus Borel remains a figure typical of these years of transition, between 1830 and 1835, and he symbolises them to perfection, with their extravagance, their bombast, and their atmosphere of melodrama. Baudelaire said of him later,[3] that there would have been something lacking in Romanticism if he had never existed, and it was to him, and not to more famous poets amongst his elders, that he turned for inspiration in his formative years. This fantastic and often absurd figure seized hold of his imagination as a young man, when he had not yet found his own personality; he sensed, beneath the theatrical gestures and the exaggerated acting of Borel's, the true nature of his inspiration, and he himself was able to achieve what his lycanthropic predecessor had only dimly conceived.

NOTES

INTRODUCTION

1. Published in Starkie: *Petrus Borel en Algérie.*
2. Published in *extenso* by Starkie: *Op. cit.*
3. *Petits Romantiques Français.*
4. *Op. cit.*

PART ONE

Chapter 1
THE EARLY YEARS

1. *Champavert*, p. 11.
2. *Ibid.*, p. 13.

Chapter 2
LE PETIT CÉNACLE

1. Quoted by Aristide Marie in *Gérard de Nerval*, p. 32.
2. *Conversations with Goethe*, p. 342. (Everymans Library.)
3. *Histoire du Romantisme.*
4. *Ibid.*

Chapter 3
LA BATAILLE D'HERNANI

1. *Mémoires d'un Bourgeois de Paris*, Vol. III, Chap. VII.
2. The account of the rehearsals comes from the *Mémoires* of Dumas, Book XIII, Chap. VII.
3. The account of the First Night of *Hernani* comes from Gautier: *Histoire du Romantisme* and from *Victor Hugo raconté par un Témoin de sa Vie.*
4. Lassailly, though not actually a Bouzingo, was similar in his extravagances. In 1833 he published his most notorious work, *Les Roueries de Trialph*, which was incomprehensible to his readers. On the title page he printed a statement of his aims.

'Ah!

Eh! hé!

Hé! hi! hi!

Oh!

Hu! hu! hu! hu!

Profession de foi de l'auteur!'

He tried to earn his living through ill-paid free-lance journalism but in 1836, having inherited a little money, he founded his own paper called *l'Ariel* to which many well-known writers contributed, amongst others Vigny, Dumas and Gautier. Like most of such reviews, it failed through lack of funds, after twenty numbers. He fell into great poverty and was obliged to remain in bed, in order to keep warm. Balzac then engaged him to help him to collect material for his novels and to discuss the plots with him, but Lassailly had to be prepared to work at any hour of the night or day. After a week he was so exhausted that he resigned his employment; he said that Balzac used to get him up out of bed seven or eight times during the night, keeping him awake on cups of black coffee. He used some of his assistant's verse for Lucien de Rubempré in his novel, *Les Illusions Perdues*. In 1840 Lassailly, having once more some money, founded another periodical, *Revue Critique*, which lasted only for four numbers. His end was like that of a Bouzingo story. He went mad, it is said, through love of an unknown woman to whom he had never spoken, whom he once saw passing in the street and whom he loved on the spot. He followed her to discover who she was. She was La Comtesse de Magnencourt, daughter of Le Comte de Tracy, son-in-law of Lafayette. He gave up all his work to be free to follow her wherever she went, and stood outside both her town and country houses. He often walked ten miles merely for a sight of her, and would leave unsigned poems and letters for her, hidden, as he informed her by message, in the hollow trunks of trees and similar places. Then, one day, he found her houses closed, both in town and in the country—she had gone away with her husband on a foreign trip. He was found wandering mad in the streets of Paris. Friends, headed by Vigny and Lamartine, obtained for him a Civil List pension, and he was placed in the mental nursing-home of Le Docteur Blanche, who was later to care for Gérard de Nerval. In 1843, when he was near his end, friends begged the Count to allow his wife to visit him. He consented and she arrived at the nursing-home, sat beside Lassailly's bed and talked to him, and, as she left, kissed him on the brow. He died happy, that night, 14th July 1843, aged thirty-six years. Vigny mentions him sympathetically in his *Journal*, and Lardanchet wrote of him in his *Les Enfants Perdus du Romantisme*.

5. Dumas: *Mémoires*, Book XIV, Chap. III.

Chapter 4
THE JULY REVOLUTION

1. Gautier: *Histoire du Romantisme*, p. 85.
2. *Madame Putiphar*, Vol. II, p. 256.

PART TWO

Chapter 1
SPLEEN

1. Une *Amitié Amoureuse*, pp. 97–98.
2. *Œuvres*, Vol. II, p. 330.
3. *Ibid.*, Vol. XVI, p. 69.
4. He is described by Dumas in his *Mémoires*; by Gérard de Nerval in *Dieux Inconnus*; by Champfleury in *Vignettes Romantiques*; by Éliphas Lévi in *Histoire de la Magie*; and by Erdan in *La France Mystique*. Caillaux, his faithful disciple, describes his thought in *L'Arche de la Nouvelle Alliance*.
5. Printed *in extenso* in Appendix I.
6. The last years of the *Mapah's* life were sad and disillusioned, when he lost faith even in himself, and began to doubt his own divinity. At the end he had only one disciple left—an old Auvergnat chestnut-roaster—and to him he entrusted the duty of propagating his gospel when he had gone. But the disciple does not seem to have carried out the injunctions of the Master, since *Évadisme* is never heard of again. The *Mapah* died some time in 1851.
7. E. de Mirécourt: *Biographie de Boccace*, p. 52.
8. *La Vie Littéraire*, Vol. III, p. 41.
9. Vid. especially in *Peau de Chagrin*.
10. *Mémoires*, Vol. I, Chap. XLIII.
11. Ch. Simond: *La Vie Française*, 1800–1900.
12. Rabbe: *Journal d'un Pessimiste*, p. 71 (Bibliothèque Romantique.)
13. *Souvenirs*, Vol. I, p. 160.

Chapter 2
CARNIVAL

1. *Paris Anecdoté*, p. 287.
2. Kracauer: *Jacques Offenbach*, p. 50.
3. d'Alton Shée has given an account of it in *Mémoires du Vicomte d'Aulnès*.
4. *L'Artiste*, January–June 1841.
5. The only reliable account of the life of Musard is an article by Alfred Pougin published in *Intermédiaire des Chercheurs et des Curieux*, June 1911.
6. *Intermédiaire des Chercheurs et des Curieux*, June 1911.
7. *Lettres Parisiennes*, Vol. I, p. 51.
8. *Ibid.*, Vol. I, p. 64.
9. *Ibid.*, Vol. I, p. 50.

10. Musard's vogue lasted a bare ten years, then his popularity began to wane, and he was never heard of again. By 1842, when Paris had become serious and respectable, his success had vanished. Then, instead of using his gains to bolster up his waning popularity, he quietly retired and lived in Auteuil in bourgeois peace and comfort on his savings, until his death in 1859.

Chapter 3
THE DANDIES

1. *Mon Cœur mis à nu.*
2. *Confessions*, Book VI.
3. *Mémoires, Première Série*, pp. 220–221.
4. *Les Soupeurs de mon Temps.*
5. D'Alton Shée: *Mémoires du Vicomte d'Aulnès.*
6. Villemessant: *Les Hommes de mon Temps*, pp. 184–5.
7. Karr: *Le Livre du Bord*, Tome I, p. 86.
8. Article called *Le Lion d'Aujourd'hui* in *La Mode*, 11/7/1840.
9. *Revue des Deux Mondes*, February 1846.
10. Poem by Jarry in *Cénacles et Vieux Logis Parisiens.*
11. Séché: *La Jeunesse dorée sous Louis Philippe.*
12. The last twenty years of Roger de Beauvoir's life were gloomy. In 1847, when he was over fifty, he married a beautiful actress from La Comédie Française, Mademoiselle Aimée-Léocadie Doze, but the marriage did not prove a happy one. Although they had three children they eventually parted, after a long and sordid lawsuit. He tried to return to his former life, but everything was too much changed. He had lost most of his fortune and his good looks, for he had grown very stout through overeating, and bald, and his clothes were now shabby. His last years were embittered through poverty, loneliness and ill-health, and there was little left of the Venetian nobleman, the Dandy of 1830. During his last six years he hardly stirred from his chair, crippled and tortured as he was by gout. Only a few faithful friends, like Barbey d'Aurevilly, ever came to see him, and when he died in 1860 he was completely forgotten.
13. *Œuvres Complètes*, (François Bernouard), Vol. X, p. 310.
14. *Ibid.*, Vol. XIV, p. 298.
15. *Ibid., ibid.*, p. 64.
16. *Ibid., ibid.*, p. 296.
17. *Ibid., ibid.*, p. 206.
18. *Ibid.*, Vol. X, p. 311.
19. *Ibid., ibid.*, p. 229.
20. *Ibid., ibid.*, p. 230.
21. Privat d'Anglemont: *Paris Anecdoté.*

PART THREE

Chapter 1
LES BOUZINGOS

1. *Histoire du Romantisme.*
2. Aristide Marie: *Gérard de Nerval,* p. 40.
3. *Revue Anecdotique,* December 1859.
4. Marc Montifaud: *Les Romantiques.*
5. *Pandæmonium. (Feu et Flamme.)*
6. *Revue Anecdotique,* December 1859.
7. Written in 1862 but published in *Œuvres en Prose,* p. 346.
8. Gautier: *Les Jeunes France. (Daniel Jovard.)*

Chapter 2
RHAPSODIES

1. *Rhapsodies,* p. 7.
2. *Ibid.,* p. 9.
3. *Champavert,* p. 15.
4. *Rhapsodies,* p. 193.
5. No copies are to be found either in the Bibliothèque Nationale or in the Bibliothèque de l'Arsenal.
6. The Collège des Quatre Nations was founded by Mazarin in 1661 for the education of 15 Italians, 15 Alsatians, 20 Flemings and 10 Roussillon men. He left it his library in his will. This eventually became the Bibliothèque Mazarine and finally became part of the Institut in 1806. The Collège lasted until the Revolution.
7. Quotation taken from Aristide Marie: *Petrus Borel,* p. 74.

Chapter 3
FEU ET FLAMME

1. The subsequent life of Philothée O'Neddy is told in Appendix II.

Chapter 4
CHAMPAVERT

1. *Champavert,* p. 35.
2. *Ibid.,* p. 83. 'very well' (*sic*) in English in the text.
3. *Ibid.,* p. 171.
4. *Ibid.,* p. 293.
5. *Ibid.,* p. 380.
6. *Ibid.,* p. 374.
7. *Ibid.,* p. 383.
8. *Ibid.,* p. 363.
9. *Ibid.,* p. 357.

Chapter 5
LA BOHÊME DU DOYENNÉ

1. Reported by Maxime Ducamp in his *Souvenirs*.
2. By Gérard de Nerval in *Premier Château de Bohême* and by Dumas in *Mémoires*.
3. *Premier Château de Bohême*.
4. Dumas: *Mémoires*.

Chapter 6
MADAME PUTIPHAR

1. Claretie: *Petrus Borel*.
2. Vid. letters published by Adolphe Julien in *Le Romantisme et l'Editeur Renduel*.
3. Published by Parran in *Romantiques*.
4. Unpublished letter, 22 February 1837.
5. Parran: *Romantiques*.
6. *Ibid., ibid.*
7. Aristide Marie has printed it after *Rhapsodies*, p. 217.
8. *Colour Studies in Paris*.
9. Vol. II, Chap. XXIII.
10. Vol. I, p. 107.
11. Vol. II, p. 306.
12. 3 June 1839.
13. Some of it must have been written by 1833 as O'Neddy quotes some lines from it in *Feu et Flamme*.

Chapter 7
SATAN

1. *Les Français peints par eux-mêmes*, Tome II.
2. *Petrus Borel*, p. 120.
3. Both Claretie and Aristide Marie state incorrectly that it was first published in *La Revue Pittoresque* in 1844. It was only reprinted there.
4. They are reprinted by Aristide Marie after *Rhapsodies*.
5. *Vignettes Romantiques*.
6. Vid. Starkie: *Petrus Borel en Algérie*, p. 7.
7. A flattering description of his work on his allotment.
8. *Le National*, 19th December 1845.
9. *Ibid.*, 24th December 1845.

PART FOUR

Chapter 2
THE INSPECTOR

1. Vid. letter published by Starkie: *Op. cit.*, p. 13.
2. *Petits Romantiques*, p. 76.
3. All the documents quoted in this part come from Starkie: *Op. cit.*
4. Letter to General Daumas, Starkie: *Op. cit.*, p. 17.
5. *Op. cit.*, p. 76.
6. Letter, 30th June 1848.
7. Claretie: *Op. cit.*, p. 114.
8. Letter, 3rd May 1849.
9. Letter, June 1850.
10. Ausone de Chancel had been a poet, of the same generation as Borel, though his poetry is more akin to that of Musset. He published several collections of verse which had some popularity; he also published poems in reviews. It was he who composed the quatrain appropriated, in varying forms, by so many other poets, and never attributed to him:

    > *On entre, on crie,*
    > *Et c'est la vie!*
    > *On baille, on sort,*
    > *Et c'est la mort!*

    His pen did not provide him with a living and, like Borel, he migrated to Algeria where he was more successful than his fellow poet. While in search for any work that would bring him some money, he had done some statistical work for the Ministry of War, and came there under the notice of General Daumas who took him with him to Algeria. He prospered there and eventually became *sous-Préfet* at Mostaganem where he and Borel met once more. He died in Algeria in 1878. Lardanchet has written of him in his *Enfants Perdus du Romantisme*.
11. Audin: *Op. cit.*, p. 77.
12. Report dated 7th October 1851.
13. *Op. cit.*, p. 78.

Chapter 3
DECLINE AND FALL

1. Letter, 29th July 1853.
2. Letter, 11th January 1854.
3. Letter, 22nd March 1855.
4. Letter, 3rd April 1855.

Chapter 4
THE DEATH OF THE WOLF

1. Letter, 25th February 1855.
2. Letter, 25th February, 1855.
3. Letter, 22nd March 1855.
4. *Op. cit.*, p. 79.
5. Letter, 28th July 1855.
6. Letter, December 1855, published in *Mercure de France*, 1/9/12.
7. Letter, 29th August 1856.
8. Given by him to René Ponsard, who gave it to Claretie, who published it in *Petrus Borel*. It has been reprinted after *Rhapsodies* by Aristide Marie.
9. Vid. unpublished letter, Starkie: *Op. cit.*, p. 13.
10. *Confessions.*
11. *Op. cit.*, p. 80.

CONCLUSION

1. *Confessions.*
2. *Champavert*, p. 31.
3. *L'Art Romantique.*

APPENDIX I

The only 'Platras' by Ganneau preserved in the Bibliothèque Nationale is the following.

BAPTÊME, MARIAGE

(Then comes a vignette made up of a woman's head and a man's head, in a circle, rising out of the sea, and intertwined initials.)

LA DOULEUR EST L'INVITATION
L'AMOUR, LA RÉVÉLATION

Il n'était que poussière et néant; une larme d'amour, tombée du sein de la mère, fait vie et lumière.

Aujourd'hui, quinze août mil huit cent trente-huit, jour de l'Assomption de la Vierge Marie et premier jour de l'Ère Évadah.

Marie n'est plus la Mère: Elle est L'ÉPOUSE:

JESUS-CHRIST n'est plus le fils: Il est L'ÉPOUX:

L'ancien monde (compression) finit:
Le nouveau monde (expansion) commence!

Les temps sont accomplis; le sacrifice d'amour est consommé;
La femme a enfanté dans la douleur son fils bien-aimé!

O MA MÈRE!

Toi qui m'as apporté la révélation du grand lingam:
Toi qui m'as dit: Marie veut dire Mariage, Évangile, Ève en Germe.

GRANDE MÈRE DE L'HUMANITÉ

Mon cœur, océan de vie, de douleur et d'amour, est la grande coupe de la nouvelle alliance où sont tombées tes larmes sacrées;
elles sont l'eau sainte du nouveau baptême,
par qui toutes les souillures sont effacées, et l'humanité sauvée!

O Marie, ils blasphèment ceux qui disent:
Que tu n'intercèdes auprès du père et du fils dans le paradis;
Ils blasphèment ceux qui disent, que tu n'es que *Sainte dans le Ciel*, impure sur
la terre oui impure! eux qui ont consacré le Dogme monstrueux du célibat
et appelé règne de Satan, œuvre de Satan, les passions humaines, qu'ils avaient frappé d'anathèmes!
LES PASSIONS: Ce sont les grandes manifestations d'Évadah, les douzes grandes table de la loi des lois (Amour) dont ta tête divine, divine épouse, est l'arche sainte.

CONSÉCRATION

Grande mère d'amour, tu m'as toi, ton fils bien-aimé, investi de ton pouvoir céleste, et par toi, Marie-Dieu, tout ce que je baptiserai et marierai sur la terre, sera baptisé et marié dans les cieux.

Tu es Marie et par toi, Marie, je marierai
Tu fus la Grande Mère; tu es aujourd'hui la Grande Épouse du Dieu-Homme de la terre, du Dieu infini de l'éternité infinie.
De tes mamelles sacrées découlera le lait de la regénération!
De ton beau sein Abeille-Reine, découlera le miel que l'humanité attend dans l'angoisse et les larmes.

A toi, Marie-Dieu, la grande investiture, le trônes des trônes, de la terre et des cieux!
Par toi, ô douce Mère, du mal est né le bien: De la mort, la vie, du péché, le salut!

Tous les sceaux théologiques sont levés, le grand mystère de l'identité, de l'unité dans la dualité, est consommé.

C'est la foi dans laquelle je mourrai et que je suis prêt à sceller de mon sang.

Cette foi je la proclame au monde!

BAPTÊME

Marie, Marie, mère,—Marie Madeleine la prostituée,—
Marie, Sainte-Vierge du Paradis!
Grande trilogie de douleur, de protestations et d'amour,

Le MAPAH VOUS SALUE, et au nom du Grand Évadah
Vous constitue et vous proclame au monde, la grande personnifi-
cation de l'unité femelle du VERBE,
Et vous baptise du nom de Marie-Ève la Génésiaque
Par ce grand Baptême, vous, toutes, mères, sœurs et fiancèes,
grands pariahs innomés, relevez-vous.
Par Marie-Ève vous etes constituées.

HOSANNAH

Jésus fils de l'homme,—Jésus le crucifié du Golgotha,
Jésus, le glorifié à la droite du Père,
Le Mapah vous salue, et, au nom du Grand Évadah, vous
constitue et vous proclame au monde, la grande personni-
fication de l'Unité mâle du verbe,
Et vous baptise du nom de Christ-Adam le Génésiaque.
Par ce Baptême, vous tous, hommes, prolétaires, parias et
grabatiers, relevez-vous!
Par Christ-Adam, vous êtes constitués!

HOSANNAH!

MARIAGE

Marie, Mère,—Marie Madeleine, la prostituée,—Marie Sainte-
Vierge du Paradis,
Grande trilogie de douleur, de protestations et d'amour.
Jésus, fils de l'homme,—Jésus, Christ du Golgotha,—
Jésus le glorifié à la droite du Père,
Le Mapah vous salue, et en face du soleil de la terre est des eaux,
du temps et de l'éternité, du fini et de l'infini.

AU NOM DU GRAND ÉVADAH

Vous constitue et vous proclame au monde, le grand symbole
la grande personnification de l'unité dans la dualité;

Et vous, Vous Marie-Ève, Unité Génésiaque femelle
vous, Christ-Adam, Unité Génésiaque mâle
Sous le nom de ANDROGYNE ÉVADAM!

Pour le grand mariage, nous, Mapah, voulons hommes, que vos mères, vos sœurs et vos fiancées, grand Pariahs, jusqu'alors innomés, apportent dans le mariage le premier terme de leur nom, et vous fiancés, le premier terme du vôtre, afin que de ces deux génériques soit constituée l'unité dans la dualité ainsi Évadam de Ève, Adam.

> Le mariage catholique romain n'est que le symbole de la consécration de l'absorbation de l'elément femelle par l'élément male.

Consacrons en outre, la préséance de la femme dans le nom Androgyne et sacré du nouveau mariage, *quia Parit in dolore* (Parce qu'elle accouche dans la douleur!)
Par les grandes fiançailles, l'humanité est constituée.
L'heure de la virilité humaine a sonné, L'Ère Évadah EST!

HOSANNAH

ÉVADAH EST GRAND

Il est dans la matière et l'esprit,
Il est l'unité dualité
Et dans tous ses termes il est l'intelligence infinie se constituant unité, amour!

AUX DEUX POLES EXPANSION, AMOUR

De notre grabat, en notre ville de Paris, la Grande Éda de la terre, le premier jour de l'an premier de l'Ère Évadah.
De notre âge, la trente-troisième année.

LE MAPAH

THE LATER LIFE OF PHILOTHÉE O'NEDDY

T he civil service killed O'Neddy as a poet, and there is little to say of him during the forty odd years which followed *Feu et Flamme*. He dropped the name of O'Neddy and reverted to his real one—Dondey de Santeney—and under that name he published stories of no great value, in various periodicals; also a short novel in the romantic vein in 1842 called *L'Anneau Enchanté, Roman de Chevalerie*. For three months in 1843 he was dramatic critic on *La Patrie*, but he resigned because the editor refused to print the flamboyant article he wrote in praise of *Les Burgraves* of Victor Hugo. For some months later in the year he was dramatic critic on *Le Courrier Français*, but the reasons of his resignation—or dismissal—are not known. He continued to write poetry intermittently until within ten years of his death, but only four sonnets were published during his lifetime. Gautier met him once in middle life, when he had not seen him since their youth together, and scarcely recognised, in the grey-haired man with his face deeply etched with wrinkles, the 'blond Othello' of 1830. He asked him then when his second volume of verse would appear, and Philothée O'Neddy answered him: 'When there are no more bourgeois!' All his remaining poems were published posthumously, by a school friend called Ernest Havet, with an Introduction, in 1877, and it is from this Introduction that we obtain the main facts of his life. This poetry is of meagre literary interest or value. Havet tells us that the most significant event of his life was a passionate love affair which is the inspiration of the *Tablettes Amoureuses*. If that is so it only inspired him to sentimentality, triviality and banality. Amongst all the other poetic effusions—*Ballades, Elégies, Visions d'un Mort Vivant, Velléités Philosophiques*—there is nothing that fulfils the promise of *Feu et Flamme*, and only one poem, the sonnet he wrote as a *post-scriptum* to *Velléités Philosophiques*, the last poem he ever wrote, is of any value or interest:

> *Or Qu'est-ce que le VRAI? Le Vrai c'est le malheur;*
> *Il souffle, et l'heur vaincu s'éteint, vaine apparence;*
> *Ses pourvoyeurs constants, le désir, l'espérance,*
> *Sous leur flamme nous font mûrir pour la douleur.*
>
> *Le Vrai, c'est l'incertain; le Vrai, c'est l'ignorance;*
> *C'est le tâtonnement dans l'ombre et dans l'erreur;*
> *C'est un concert de fête avec un fond d'horreur;*
> *C'est le neutre, l'oubli, le froid, l'indifférence.*
>
> *C'est le pauvre insulté jusque dans sa vertu;*
> *C'est au pied des tyrans l'homme libre abattu;*
> *C'est d'un amour trahi l'angoisse inexprimable.*
>
> *C'est Peut-être. A quoi bon? Qu'importe? Je ne sai,*
> *Pourquoi? Comment? Ou donc? Voilà, voilà le Vrai.*
> *Ah! le VRAI n'est pas beau, le VRAI n'est pas aimable!*

After 1846 nothing more was heard of Philothée O'Neddy in the literary world for twenty years until the revival of *Hernani* in 1867. Auguste Vacquerie, the brother of Victor Hugo's dead son-in-law, relates how a respectable elderly bourgeois came to the offices of the organising committee to obtain a free ticket for the First Night. When asked for his name he gave that of Philothée O'Neddy, famous at the *Bataille d'Hernani* nearly forty years before, and Vacquerie hastened to comply with his request, thinking it only right that the man who had struck a blow on the day of the battle should now be a witness of the final apotheosis.

Théophile Dondey lived out the days of his life in quiet obscurity in Paris with his widowed mother and spinster sister. He never married. His mother died in 1861, after being bedridden with paralysis for five years. After her death he continued to live with his elderly sister. She did not make up to him for the loss of his mother whom he loved better than any other human being. 'The chasm which has suddenly opened between my sister and me,' he wrote to his friend Havet, 'will never be filled. We can clasp hands over it, but that is all!' Dondey himself was largely to blame for the lack of intimacy and understanding between his sister and himself, for the 'je ne sais quoi de tacite, de neutre et de morne' between them, since he had always kept her from contact with real life. 'From her earliest youth' he said to Havet 'it was easy for me to realise that my sister would not marry. I resolved then to do my utmost so that her spinsterhood should be peaceful and dignified. I thought—and still think—that it is fitting for the dignity and calm of the distressing state of old-maid to surround it with a monastic atmosphere. I did my best to keep away from her, either in conversation, or in books, the full forces of life, even when they were noble and pure.' It was small wonder that there was eventually between them nothing but 'silence and shadow'. She tried at first to find consolation in painting, but art disappointed her as it had her brother, who had written earlier:

> *Triste Muse! il nous sied—sans plainte ni témoin—*
> *D'attendre la vieillesse et la mort—dans mon coin.*

In 1873 he too was struck down by paralysis and was nursed with great devotion by his sister until his death. Illness is said to have changed the peaceful, law-abiding bourgeois, and he became gloomy, bitter and violent in his views. Maybe it only released the hidden fires which he had kept damped down since his youth, but they burned now only with a destructive flame which gave neither heat nor light. Those who came into contact with him, at the end, said that his character had suddenly become radically changed. Perhaps it had only been stripped of its covering of respectability and convention. He died in 1875 in the sixty-fifth year of his age.

Appendix III

UNPUBLISHED LETTERS
BY PETRUS BOREL

———————————⧫———————————

T here are very few letters extant from the pen of Petrus Borel—besides those which he wrote from Algeria to his local superiors and to the Ministry of War in Paris, and which have been published by Starkie in *Petrus Borel en Algérie* in 1950. Two letters to Philothée O'Neddy were published by Parran in *Romantiques* in 1885; one to Renduel by Adolphe Julien in *Le Romantism et l'Editeur Renduel* in 1897; two to Balzac by Aristide Marie in *Petrus Borel* in 1922; and two to Francis Wey by Jean Richer in *Le Mercure de France* on 1st August 1952.

There are, to my knowledge, four further unpublished letters. One addressed to Philothée O'Neddy, which is printed below, comes from Nadard papers in the Bibliothèque Nationale in Paris. The other three—one of them addressed to the editor Ollivier, and the other two to the editor Renduel—are in private hands, and their owner, at the last moment, has refused permission to publish them here.

BOREL TO O'NEDDY

Au lieu de t'envoyer seulement ces quelques lignes, mon cher O'Neddy, je comptais t'expédier pour l'occasion présente un peu de copie pour l' imprimerie; mais hier j'ai eu un spleen si parfaitement insupportable, j'étais dans un marasme si profond, qu'il a été impossible de faire même le travail maunel de recopier mon petit bout de chapitre XVII—je tiens toutefois de te faire passer dans les premiers jours de la semaine prochaine,—je t'en dis pas long aujourd'hui, je n'ai plus qu'une minute à moi, on m'attend. Adieu mon brave, aime-moi toujours et je ferai de même à ton cher égard.—Tout le monde te souhaite mille biens et meilleur santé.

Petrus.

Au Bas-Baizil ce 28 avril 1837.

Appendix IV

BIBLIOGRAPHY

A. PUBLISHED WORKS BY PETRUS BOREL

1832 *Rhapsodies* (Levavasseur).

1833 *Champavert* (Renduel).

1836 *L'Obélisque de Louqsor* (Dondey-Dupré).

1836 *Robinson Crusoe* (Translation). (Francisque Borel and Alexandre Varennes.)

1838 *Comme quoi Napoléon n'a jamais exist*é (Francisque Borel and Alexandre Varennes).

1839 *Madame Putiphar* (Ollivier).

1922 Five poems by Borel, published in *L'Artiste* in 1844, also *Léthargie de la Muse*, republished by Aristide Marie at the end of his edition of *Rhapsodies*.

1927 *Le Trésor de la Caverne d'Arcueil* (La Connaissance). (Reprinted from *La Revue de Paris*, April 1843.)

B. CONTRIBUTIONS TO VARIOUS REVIEWS WHICH HAVE NOT BEEN REPRINTED

1833 'Les Pressentimens, Médianoche' (Short story). (*Album de la Mode*, No. 59.)

1834 'Anne de Bretagne' (*Le Livre de Beauté*).

1835 'Promenade en Espagne' (*Journal des Demoiselles*).

1835 'Jérôme Chasseboeuf' (*L'Artiste* Tome VII).

1839 'Jeanniquette' (Short story). (*La Presse*, July.)

1840 'Le Croque-Mort' (*Les Français Peints par eux-mêmes* Tome IV).

1841 'Le Gniaffe' (*Ibid.*, Tome IV).

1841 'Le Capitaine François de Civile' (*Le Commerce*, 8th and 9th June).

1842 'Miss Hazel' (Short story). (*L'Artiste*.)

1843 'Daphné' (*Messager*, November).

1843 'Gottfried Wolfgang' (Short story). (*La Sylphide*, Tome VIII.)

1844 'La Famille Wakefield' (*La Revue Parisienne*, Tome IX).

1844 'Le Vert Galant' (*L'Artiste*, October).

1844 'De la Chaussure chez les Anciens' (*L'Artiste*, Tome II).

1845 'Le Général Marceau et Clémence Isaure' (*L'Artiste*, May).

1845 'De la Pantoufle' (*L'Artiste*, June).

1845 'Philologie Humoristique' (*L'Artiste*, July).

1845 'Pierre Beyle' (*L'Artiste*, August).

1845 'Rêveries Ethnologiques' (*L'Artiste*, September).

1845 'Alger, son Avenir Littéraire' (*L'Artiste*, November).

1845 'Le Fou et le Roi de Suède' (*Le Commerce*, December).

1846 'Quelques Mois chez les Amazoulous' (*Journal des Chasseurs*, September).

1847 'Du Jugement Publicque' (*L'Artiste*).

1847 'Algérie, Colonisation' (*Revue de l'Orient et d'Algérie*).

Various articles in *La Liberté, Journal des Arts* between September 1832 and February 1832. Also various articles in *Le Satan* between 14th February and 8th September 1844.

C. WORKS ON PETRUS BOREL

J. Claretie: *Petrus Borel, le Lycanthrope*, 1865.

A. Marie: *Petrus Borel*, 1922.

E. Starkie: *Petrus Borel en Algérie*, 1950.

D. WORKS CONTAINING PORTIONS DEALING WITH PETRUS BOREL

C. Asselineau: *Bibliographie Romantique*, 1864.

J. L. Audin: *Petits Romantiques Français*, 1949.

C. Baudelaire: *Art Romantique*, 1868.

J. Champfleury: *Vignettes Romantiques*, 1883.

E. des Essarts: *Les Voyages de l'Esprit*, 1869.

T. Gautier: *Histoire du Romantisme*, 1872.

A. Julien: *Le Romantisme et l'Editeur Renduel*, 1897.

M. de Montifaud: *Les Romantiques*, 1878.

A. Parran: *Romantiques*, 1881.

E. WORKS USEFUL FOR A STUDY OF THE BACKGROUND OF THE PERIOD

E. d'Alton Shée: *Mémoires du Vicomte d'Aulnès*, 1868.

J. Boulanger: *Les Dandies*, 1907.

A. Dumas: *Mémoires*, 1854.

T. Gautier: *Les Jeunes France*, 1833.

Ibid., *Histoire du Romantisme*, 1872.

A. Houssaye: *Confessions*, 1885–1891.

L. Maigron: *Le Romantisme et la Mode*, 1910.

Ibid., *Le Romantisme et les Mœurs*, 1911.

M. Praz: *The Romantic Agony*, 1925.

A. Privat d'Anglemont: *Paris Anecdoté*, 1854.

L. Séché: *La Jeunesse dorée sous Louis-Philippe*, 1910.

C. Simond: *La Vie Française, 1800–1900*, 1900.

P. Véron: *Mémoires d'un Bourgeois de Paris*, 1853.

H. de Villemessant: *Mémoires d'un Journaliste*, 1884.

INDEX

B438

CS	DEWEY		VOLUMES	PARTS	COPY	EDITION	YEAR	AU
B731XS					1		1954 STARKIE	

CUTTER

PETRUS BO

CUTTER   DEWEY   CUTTER   VOLUMES   PARTS   EDITION   YEAR

```
0 0 0 0 0 0 0 0 0 0 0 0 0 0 0 0 0 0 0 0 0 0 0 0 0 0 0 0 0 0 0 0 0 0 0 0 0 0 0 0
1 1 1 1 1 1 1 1 1 1 1 1 1 1 1 1 1 1 1 1 1 1 1 1 1 1 1 1 1 1 1 1 1 1 1 1 1 1 1 1
2 2 2 2 2 2 2 2 2 2 2 2 2 2 2 2 2 2 2 2 2 2 2 2 2 2 2 2 2 2 2 2 2 2 2 2 2 2 2 2
3 3 3 3 3 3 3 3 3 3 3 3 3 3 3 3 3 3 3 3 3 3 3 3 3 3 3 3 3 3 3 3 3 3 3 3 3 3 3 3
4 4 4 4 4 4 4 4 4 4 4 4 4 4 4 4 4 4 4 4 4 4 4 4 4 4 4 4 4 4 4 4 4 4 4 4 4 4 4 4
5 5 5 5 5 5 5 5 5 5 5 5 5 5 5 5 5 5 5 5 5 5 5 5 5 5 5 5 5 5 5 5 5 5 5 5 5 5 5 5
6 6 6 6 6 6 6 6 6 6 6 6 6 6 6 6 6 6 6 6 6 6 6 6 6 6 6 6 6 6 6 6 6 6 6 6 6 6 6 6
7 7 7 7 7 7 7 7 7 7 7 7 7 7 7 7 7 7 7 7 7 7 7 7 7 7 7 7 7 7 7 7 7 7 7 7 7 7 7 7
8 8 8 8 8 8 8 8 8 8 8 8 8 8 8 8 8 8 8 8 8 8 8 8 8 8 8 8 8 8 8 8 8 8 8 8 8 8 8 8
9 9 9 9 9 9 9 9 9 9 9 9 9 9 9 9 9 9 9 9 9 9 9 9 9 9 9 9 9 9 9 9 9 9 9 9 9 9 9 9
```

70
71
74
75
76
77
79
83
85